CASSANDRA SPEAKS

ALSO BY ELIZABETH LESSER

Marrow

Broken Open

The Seekers Guide

CASSANDRA

WHEN WOMEN ARE THE STORYTELLERS,

THE HUMAN STORY CHANGES

SPEAKS

ELIZABETH LESSER

HARPER WAVE

An Imprint of HarperCollinsPublishers

HarperCollins books may be purchased for educational, business, or sales promotional use. For information, please email the Special Markets Department at SPsales@harpercollins.com.

Excerpt on page 96 from "Were the First Artists Mostly Women?" by Virginia Hughes, Copyright 2013 by *National Geographic*. Reprinted with permission. Excerpt on page 197 from the 2010 TED Talk, by Tony Porter, "A Call To Men." Reprinted with permission. To watch the full talk, visit TED.com. Excerpt on page 129 from Scott Jeffrey https://scottjeffrey .com/shadow-work/. Reprinted with permission. Excerpt on page 157 from Carlos A. Ball blog post. Used with permission. *Pygmalion and Galatea* by Jean-Léon Gérôme. *Adam and Eve* by Lucas Cranach the Elder used with permission of Art Heritage / Alamy Stock Photo.

FIRST EDITION

Designed by Bonni Leon-Berman
MDogan/Shutterstock.com (Sophia)
D-T/Shutterstock.com (Buddha)

Library of Congress Cataloging-in-Publication Data
Names: Lesser, Elizabeth, author.
Title: Cassandra speaks: when women are the storytellers, the human story changes / Elizabeth Lesser.
Description: First edition. | New York, NY: HarperCollins, [2020] | Summary: "In her new book, bestselling author Elizabeth Lesser looks to the stories told about women over the ages and how they contribute to persistent misogyny and gender inequality, and offers a path towards framing new stories that honor all people"—Provided by publisher.
Identifiers: LCCN 2020025794 (print) | LCCN 2020025795 (ebook) | ISBN 9780062887184 (hardcover) | ISBN 9780062887207 (epub)
Subjects: LCSH: Feminism. | Women in literature. | Sex role in literature. | Storytelling—Social aspects. | Misogyny. | Sexism. | Equality.
Classification: LCC HQ1155 .L468 2020 (print) | LCC HQ1155 (ebook) | DDC 305.42—dc23
LC record available at https://lccn.loc.gov/2020025794
LC ebook record available at https://lccn.loc.gov/2020025795

20 21 22 23 24   LSC   10 9 8 7 6 5 4 3 2 1

For

Rahmiel and Eve

Daniel and Taylor

Michael and Rebecca

and the next generation

you are raising

What will the writing of history be like, when the definition is shared equally by men and women? Will we devalue the past, overthrow the categories, supplant order with chaos? No—we will simply step out under the free sky. We will observe how it changes, how the stars rise and the moon circles, and we will describe the earth and its workings in male and female voices. . . . We now know that man is not the measure of that which is human, but men and women are. This insight will transform consciousness as decisively as Copernicus' discovery that the earth is not the center of the universe.

—GERDA LERNER

CONTENTS

INTRODUCTION

This is a book about stories—the stories a culture tells, and how those stories become the culture. It's about the stories we still blindly cling to, and the ones that cling to us: the origin tales, the guiding myths, the religious parables, the stories passed down through the centuries about women and men, power and war, sex and love, and the values by which we live. Stories written mostly by men, yet with lessons and laws for all of humanity. We have outgrown so many of them, and still they endure. This book is about those old stories, and it's about what happens when women are the storytellers, too—when we speak from our authentic voices, when we flex our values, when we become protagonists in the tales we tell about what it means to be human.

And so, I will start with a story. It takes place on a summer day, at Omega Institute, the education and retreat center I cofounded right out of college. Today, Omega is a thriving institution, offering hundreds of workshops and conferences every year on its campus in upstate New York. At the time of my story, I was the only woman in leadership at Omega. I was also a harried single mother, juggling work and parenting, trying to squeeze the impossible into each day.

There's a room in Omega's dining hall where faculty can share a meal and mingle ideas. On any given day, there's an eclectic mix of innovative thinkers in that room—from medical researchers to indigenous healers, from yogis to scientists, and from NBA basketball players to Nobel Peace Prize winners. On this day, I was surrounded by speakers and teachers having fascinating conversations, but instead of chatting with them about breakthroughs in cancer care or mindfulness meditation or sports psychology, I was engaged in a familiar debate with my two little boys. I wanted them to eat a healthy lunch; they wanted to pedal their bikes down to the country store to buy fried chicken and ice-cream cones.

The boys won the debate and ran gleefully out into the summer day. By then almost everyone else had finished lunch and left the room. But in the corner, bent over a book and slurping cream of something soup, was one straggler—a woman with short gray hair and thick reading glasses, a university Classics professor who was part of a conference exploring the power of myth in modern culture. She had just published a book—a retelling of ancient legends from the point of view of the women in the tales. I had not yet read it. It was one of many books stacked on my bedside table, a common phenomenon for people who love to read but also have children and a job.

I was about to leave the faculty dining room when I noticed something disconcerting. The woman in the corner, the Classics professor, was so lost in reading that she was absentmindedly dribbling soup on the front of her sweater—but actually, it was my sweater. I had offered it to her the evening before, when we met for the first time at a faculty orientation. You look cold, I had said, and she nodded and took the sweater without a word in response. What an odd person, I thought. Now I sat watching her, and my sweater, spellbound.

Sensing my eyes on her, the professor looked up and motioned to me. She pointed to the chair across the table from her. I went over, sat down, and within minutes, I would not have cared if she had dumped a whole tureen of soup on my sweater, because she told me a story that turned out to be the answer to a question I didn't even know I was asking. The story got under my skin and stayed with me. It set in motion a cascade of critical choices I would make over the next few years—choices that would help me reclaim my voice, my courage, my self-worth.

Our conversation began lightly enough. I asked the professor if her room was pleasant, if she was sleeping well, how her class was going. "Fine, fine, fine," she mumbled, waving away each question with her soupspoon. Then she lifted her eyes and peered at me.

"And how is your *life* going?" she asked.

"Not so well!" I was surprised to hear myself divulge. Suddenly, I was telling this strange stranger about a meeting I'd been in earlier that day, and not just that meeting, but situations I found myself in over and over at work. I told her how frustrated I was as a woman leader, how it was like speaking a second language, how I was learning that language as fast as I could, but the guys I worked with didn't seem interested in learning my language, understanding my insights, enacting my priorities. I could see some important changes the organization needed to make. I could see what would happen if we didn't make those changes. But no one listened. Occasionally, something I had unsuccessfully argued for would resurface as someone else's brilliant idea. I spent my days either capitulating or complaining. I didn't like who I was becoming.

"All I do is complain," I told the professor. "I'm pissed off all the time. No one listens to me. l feel kind of crazy."

The professor took another slurp of soup. Then she put down her spoon and sat quietly for a few moments. "I have been thinking a lot about Cassandra," she finally said. "You remember her, of course."

"Barely," I admitted.

"Well, then, I'll remind you. Cassandra was a princess from the city of Troy. She was the most beautiful of King Priam and Queen Hecuba's daughters. As such, she had many suitors, both mortal and immortal." The professor looked around the empty room and then lowered her voice, as if including me in some ancient gossip. "Zeus, king of the gods, was after Cassandra. And so was his son, Apollo. To woo her, Apollo gave her something only a god could give—the coveted gift of seeing into the future. But when he tried to seduce her, Cassandra refused his sexual advances. This enraged Apollo. Instead of just taking the gift of prophecy away, he grabbed her, spat in her mouth, and put a curse on her. 'You will remain clairvoyant, Cassandra,' he said, 'but now, no one will listen to you, no one will believe your predictions.' So, no matter what she foresaw—from the sacking of Troy, to the death of her brothers, to the multiple tragedies that would befall her people—no one believed Cassandra. She was eventually driven mad by knowing the truth and being doubted when she spoke it. Her final indignity came at the end of the Trojan War. As her city lay in ruins—just as she had prophesized—she was abducted and raped by a Greek warrior."

As the professor spun me the tale of Cassandra, I began to feel less and less as if she was speaking about characters from a

Greek myth, and more and more as if she was speaking about women in general, in ancient times and our times. Finally, she said, "Listen here, young lady. Women have been ignored, ridiculed, punished, even killed for their opinions forever. But without the balancing power of her voice—the female voice— things in this world end in disaster. Cassandra's tale is your tale. It is all of our tales. We must speak, and we must be taken seriously. We must change the way the story ends."

"But how?" I asked, my voice rising, thinking about the meeting I had been in that morning. "I try, but they don't listen to me."

The professor gave me the side-eye. "Your tone right now? That's the first step. Stop whining. Are you going to be a doomed prophetess, or are you going to find a different voice and save your city?"

"Well, that sounds a little overblown! I run a conference center. These are not life-or-death issues."

"Ah, but they are! It doesn't matter where you work, what you do, where you live. Women know something that the world needs now. We know it in our bones. We've always known it."

"Yeah," I answered. "That sounds good, but—"

"Shhhh!" The woman put her finger to her lips. "Listen," she whispered. "Listen to Cassandra." Now she looked less like a professor from a prestigious university and more like a benevolent witch from a fairy tale. She reached across the lunch table and put her hand on my hand. "When Cassandra speaks, we must listen. There's work to do. Listen to her, and then get to work." She patted my hand, stood up, ran a napkin over her chest—smearing the soup into my sweater—and left the dining room.

I never saw the sweater again. I never saw the professor again. And I never forgot the story of Cassandra. From then on—during crises and crossroads at work, or whenever it was time for me to step up and take a risk for what I believed in, for what I knew to be right—I conjured up Cassandra. I called on her to help me find my voice, to trust my values, and to change the way the story ends. I have been calling on her ever since, in my own life, and as a prayer for the world. I know, *in my bones*, that we can break Cassandra's curse, that we can dispel our culture's enduring mistrust and devaluing of women. And when we do, all of humanity will benefit.

In the past few years, I have thought of Cassandra's story almost every day as more and more women demand to be heard and trusted. I have thought about other stories, too, ancient and modern ones, a whole brew of stories that people have been absorbing for centuries. Stories that tell false and destructive narratives about women and men, femininity and masculinity, and the nature and purpose of life. Stories we would be wise to scrap, and to replace with healthier ones.

Part I of this book, "Origin Stories," explores some of the old tales, starting with Adam and Eve, the most influential couple in Western culture. Here's a mini-refresher of our prevailing origin story: In the beginning, life was great in the garden of Eden, until God noticed that Adam needed a helpmate, and so he made Eve, the first woman. Then Eve got curious, listened to a snake, seduced Adam into disobeying God, and everything after that went downhill. *The Fall*. That's the foundation, the one that sets all the others up, the first story to paint womankind as "second in creation, and first to sin." That tagline brands our culture—it's our DNA, it informs our daily lives, it lives in our bodies. To give you a taste of the legacy passed down to us from Adam and Eve, here are three quotes from writings I explore in greater detail in Part I.

From Tertullian, an early Christian writer, often called the founder of Western theology:

> In pain shall you bring forth children, woman, and you shall turn to your husband and he shall rule over you. And do you not know that you are Eve? God's sentence hangs still over all your sex and His punishment weighs down upon you. You are the devil's gateway; you are she who first violated the forbidden tree and broke the law of God. Because of you, even the Son of God had to die.

From Ecclesiasticus, an early biblical book of morals:

> A gift from the Lord is a silent wife,
> And nothing is so precious as her self-discipline.
> Charm upon charm is a wife with a sense of shame,
> And nothing is more valuable than her bound-up mouth.

And this one, from the Mishnah, a sacred Jewish compendium of laws:

> To the woman God gave nine curses: the burden of the blood of menstruation and the blood of virginity; the burden of pregnancy; the burden of childbirth; the burden of bringing up the children; her head is covered

as one in mourning; she pierces her ear like a permanent slave; she is not to be believed as a witness.

That one really gets me—how menstruation and childbirth and parenting are all seen as burdens as opposed to examples of strength, worthiness, and power, whereas the physicality and roles granted to men are vaulted into god-like attributes. This is where it all started. And that last bit: "she is not to be believed as a witness"—this ancient indictment is echoed throughout history. It can be found in stories from the Bible to the Greek myths to the fairy tales we read to children and the literature we study in schools. It is Cassandra's story, and it is the story of any woman who has been dismissed, gaslighted, or punished for having an opinion of her own. It is the old trope of the hysterical girl or the scorned woman who is not to be believed as a witness to her own experience.

But here's the good news: while the distrust of women is the root of the story, it no longer has to be the fruit.

✳

Part II of this book is about women and power. It's about redefining what it means to be courageous, daring, and strong. It's about taking back words and making them our own. It's about doing power differently.

The summer that author Toni Morrison died, I went on a binge-read of her majestic novels and essays. For years, she had been a beacon for me: a truth teller, a way finder, a culture changer. A woman who bore witness to her own experience and courageously told her story. I remember the first time I saw her interviewed by Oprah Winfrey on television in 1996. She had already won the Pulitzer Prize, the American Book Award, and the Nobel Prize in Literature, but it was obvious just looking at the way she held herself, listening to her whispery-soft yet dignified voice, that she didn't need any of those prizes to know her own worth. She told Oprah, "I've always known I was gallant."

I was struck by the use of that word, *gallant*. Not a word that women usually use to describe themselves, but when I heard her say "I've always known I was gallant," I felt my backbone straighten, and my head rise, and I understood how Toni Morrison had found the courage to tell the stories that lived in her bones, and to write her groundbreaking books.

GALLANT: From the old French, meaning, "chivalrous; dashing; brave; noble-minded: a gallant knight; a gallant rescue attempt."

Gallant is what Toni Morrison was. And it's what she did: she made a gallant rescue attempt for the soul of humanity.

I keep a basket of quotes on my writing desk. I'm always adding to it—beautiful lines from poets, mind-blowing bits from scientists, motivation from activists, quiet wisdom from spiritual teachers. Every morning when I sit down to work, I randomly pick a quote and I use it all day to lift me up—to clear my head of petty thinking, to give me the courage to speak my truth, to lift Cassandra's curse from my own tongue. On the day that Toni Morrison died, I went looking in that basket for words from her. I pulled a few quotes out and spread them out on my desk, and this is the one that called to me: "As you enter positions of trust and power," Toni Morrison wrote, "dream a little before you think."

As you enter positions of trust and power, dream a little before you think. There's a lot packed into that one line. Every time I read it, I hear Toni Morrison's voice. I hear her telling me to respect my own dreams and to trust my instincts before I allow self-doubt and overthinking to highjack my vision. Her words remind me that throughout the ages, women have been taught to be distrustful of our dreams, to dismiss them as second-rate, or soft, or emotionally overwrought. We've been told we talk too much, share too much, feel too much. That we cannot be trusted in the realms of power and influence. As we enter positions of trust and power—at work, in our creative ventures, in our relationships—we get the message *not* to dream our dreams, but instead to fit ourselves into the old dreams, the old stories, and into the way it's always been done.

But Toni Morrison did the opposite. Her books were lightning bolts of nonconformity and courage. They leaped where no American books had gone before. They took their place at the literary table that for centuries had been set only for white people and for men. They spoke in a different cadence. They untwisted the truth so that whole swaths of people who had been stripped of their gallantry were given it back. Toni Morrison told a truer narrative, and in doing so the meager foundations of Western storytelling began to crumble.

When the stories that have glued together a culture lose their potency, things begin to fall apart, but new things rise up. Turmoil and backlash ensue, but so do big leaps forward. This is the clumsy way that human cultures evolve. We are living in a time when the stories that have provided meaning and structure for Western customs and institutions are being challenged. Some of those stories are beautiful, instructive, and worth saving. But many of our foundational narratives that pretend to be about and for all of us were told by only a few of us, and therefore have served a mere slice of humanity. They have set in stone which values and temperaments should prevail, what power looks like, and who gets to have it.

For all the many strides women have made, the old stories haunt us still: religious tales where the women are fickle, or weak, or cursed; fairy tales where the men are white knights and swashbuckling saviors, bad boys and lone wolves, warriors and kings. And where the women are ugly hags and scullery maids, or sleeping beauties and girls locked in towers. Then there are the famous novels where the women get to be one of two archetypes—the Madonna or the whore; the helpless damsel, or the too-strong, too-tough, too-much woman. Perfection or damnation. When you make a study of a wide range of the old stories, it is stunning to see how many of them serve as warnings against women doing "unfeminine" things, like speaking, or claiming autonomy over our bodies and sexuality, or being gallant. The stories steer men toward what is coded masculine: stoicism, warriorship, and violence. They forewarn men against anything coded feminine: the home, the hearth, the heart, the "womanly arts" of empathy and care. So much of the sorry state of our world hangs on the excess of the so-called masculine virtues in our guiding storylines. So much was lost with the disparaging of anything coded feminine and the erasure of women as protagonists and heroes.

This overemphasis on masculinity is what is called patriarchy. It's not my favorite word, *patriarchy*, but I haven't found a better one. It's not my favorite word because it has the effect of lumping all men together into one camp, and all women in another, and if you dig a little beneath the surface of each man and each woman you will discover the obvious truth that men are a varied bunch of humans, as are women. To empower the lost voices and undervalued ways of women is not an either/ or, oppositional proposition. Rather, it is an act of restoration, a righting of a world seriously out of whack.

It feels to me both the right time and a fraught time to be writing a book about women and men, femininity and masculinity. The right time, because all around us women are rising up and overturning old concepts and structures; fraught, because of the wide gaps that exist between women everywhere—gaps in our privileges, our generations, our rights, our beliefs. Some women will not see themselves in the ways in which I have experienced being a woman. Other women—and men, too—will relate to the whole notion of gender in a more fluid way. The variety of women in the world makes grouping all of us into one category a complicated matter. I am aware that any examination of women is an intersectional one—I know that other thinkers and writers are exploring more deeply than I how sexism, racism, homophobia, xenophobia, and classism are interconnected.

When speaking of women as a group, we run into the same challenges as when we speak of any category of people: within a group—racial, ethnic, political, religious, gay, straight, young, old—there is both commonality and diversity. Women around the world and even one block over are different from one another due to a myriad of reasons. But even with our differences, and regardless of how we identify ourselves along the spectrum of gender, women still share many similarities—some from nature, some from nurture, and some from the wounds of patriarchy. One of those wounds is the tendency, drilled into women for millennia, to doubt who we are, to diminish what we value, to have contempt for our bodies, for our very selves. And this doubt—this shame and reticence—can be traced all the way back to those old stories.

I'm not saying anything revelatory when I remind us that the people in charge for most of human history have been men, and a certain type of man, brandishing a specific version of masculinity. And for most of these years, the world over, women were expected to stay in a narrow lane: mother, caregiver, keeper of the hearth, mender of the hearts, cleaner-uppers of the mess. The old stories solidified those roles so much so that over the ages, gender differences have been carved not only into our cultural norms but also into the grooves in our brains. And because of this—because of how womanhood has been defined and regulated, and also because of biology and physiology—women carry within us a certain way of being, thinking, feeling, and leading long denied its validity and power, and now urgently needed.

It's a big ol' soup, this question of women in our times, and often I have wanted to step away from the stove and leave the cooking to others—to the academics, or the activists, or the next generation of thinkers and leaders. But I have a specific take on the questions at hand, gleaned from my years of looking at them holistically—from the historical to the personal, from the psychological to the transcendent. I do not claim to have the final word. I write from my experience and research; I add it to the mix. I do this because I believe these are important times. Humanity has come to the end of a long, unbalanced era, one that started thousands of years ago, one that has been both creative and destructive, but one that has run its course and is running away with our future.

I often think back to that lunch in the Omega faculty dining room and to what the Classics professor told me. "It doesn't matter where you work, what you do, where you live," she said. "Women know something that the world needs now. We know it in our bones. We've always known it." I believe it is time for women to dig deep, to excavate our voices, to elevate our emotional and relational intelligence, and to transcend the limiting stories of the past. It is time for us to be the scribes and the teachers of a new way—to "dream a little before we think," as Toni Morrison said—and to stitch the world back together through care and inclusion.

Part III of this book offers some ideas and practices to help you spark and ennoble your own dreams.

When I dream of a better world, I dream of men fearlessly reclaiming words and traits that have been coded feminine: feelings, empathy, communication. I dream of women reclaiming traits that have been coded masculine: ambition, confidence, authority. But what I dream of most is women and men mixing it up, blending it all together, tempering power with wisdom, giving muscle and prestige to love and nurture. That's my dream. I hope this book gives voice to yours and helps you weave the new stories the world is waiting for.

PART I

ORIGIN STORIES

History isn't what happened. It's who tells the story.

—*Sally Roesch Wagner*

What's the best thing about getting older? Certainly not my creaky knees, or the way my whole body is proving the existence of gravity, or how I often find myself standing in the middle of a room wondering what I'm looking for. No, the best thing about being older is that I finally trust my own point of view, so much so that I no longer suppress it when it deserves to be expressed, nor do I argue it with a person who is uninterested in listening, learning, or growing (or helping me listen, learn, or grow). I know my own heart, and I value my experience. I am not afraid of being exposed when I'm wrong. I'm not looking for accolades when I do the right thing. I am at home in my own skin, and my own mind, and in the joy and mess of being human.

I wasn't always like this. As a girl and a young woman in my early career years, and in my first marriage, I didn't know my own mind, treasure my own body, or trust my emotions. I didn't trust myself. Well, sometimes I did. Sometimes I spoke my truth, but lurking always in the background was self-doubt and a vague sense of shame.

Where did that doubt and shame come from? Why did I question my basic validity as a human being? Why did I devalue my interests and perspectives and rights? Why was I ashamed of my body? I didn't know. I didn't even realize I had shame. I just knew there were acceptable ways to be a woman—like being nice and agreeable, and not overly aggressive or overtly ambitious. If I felt desire for pleasure or an instinct for power, then I was wrong to feel that way. And if I dared to follow those desires and instincts, I was bad. I knew this because I was dipped in the waters of our culture, just as everyone else was, hearing the same stories and absorbing the same rules.

Even as a girl I understood there was something out of line about being female—something physical, something emotional, something sexual that made me, and the whole lot of us girls and women, suspect, untrustworthy, punishable. I was an imaginative and gutsy little girl, born into a family that consisted of a creative, self-centered, and domineering father; a smart, submissive, and pissed-off mother; and four daughters. My mother—a frustrated writer and a high school English teacher—read to her girls from a wide range of literature: Greek myths, Bible stories, Homer's *Odyssey*, *The Adventures of Huckleberry Finn*, Grimm's fairy tales, *Little Women*. From these texts, and from observing my parents, I drank the cultural Kool-Aid. I metabolized the preferred range of human behaviors. The noble characters in the books we read had qualities like quick thinking, curtailed emotions, rugged individualism, and a competitive nature. They did not exhibit what my father called the "girly stuff"—excessive feeling and concern about the feelings of other people. Excessive chattering. Excessive need for someone to chatter back. General excessiveness all around. My father wasn't the only one dismissing the girly stuff and elevating his own ways of being. My mother upheld his ways, too, even as she strained against them.

I dragged what I learned in childhood into adulthood and

marriage and the work world and discovered the same narrow range of heralded humanness wherever I went. When my so-called girly stuff rose to the surface at home or work—when in a meeting I would be brought to tears (instead of responding with locker-room put-downs or poker-faced stoicism), when I wanted to talk about what I was feeling in my marriage, when I felt belittled and scared by sexual innuendo and outright harassment, when the competition and violence in the world offended something deep inside of me—I would judge *myself.* Too emotional, too needy, too sexually tempting, too naive and idealistic. Best to tamp down those qualities and behaviors if I wanted peace at home and achievement at work and influence in the world. Best to fit myself into the already acceptable mold, because that was "just the way it is."

I can't point to one thing that finally emboldened me to trust in the legitimacy of my self—a self that is broad enough, complex enough, and unique enough to contain all of who I am. My tenderness *and* my ambition, my empathy *and* my individuality. My femaleness, my maleness, my genderless-ness. Such clumsy words, all of them. All in need of rounding out. All I know is that in my early thirties I became acutely aware of the feelings of constriction, heartache, and anger that had been brewing in me since I was a girl. Slowly, the desire to do something to change the story became stronger than my fear of speaking up. Maybe it was the wave of women gathering their strength all over the world that amped up my courage and freed my voice. Or maybe my meditation practice was paying off, giving me a strong backbone and a way of regarding myself and others with calm curiosity. Or was it my first, clumsy attempts at being in therapy that helped me unravel the stories that had shaped me? Probably all of the above. They all woke me up. I began to know in my bones that "just the way it is" was actually just a story—a story with ancient roots; a story that begged to be revisited and revamped.

And so, I went back into those teaching tales that my mother had read to her girls—Adam and Eve and other Bible parables, the Greek and Roman myths, Shakespeare's tragedies, war stories and heroic legends. I had absorbed those stories as if they were about humankind, about men *and* women. But here's the thing: stories created only by men are really stories about men. I wanted to explore what would have happened—and what can happen now—when women are the storytellers, too.

Whether we know it or not, whether we have read them or not, whether we believe them or don't, our daily lives take direction from stories that are hundreds, even thousands of years old. I was reminded of this the other day when I read a news story about the assistant principal and athletic director of a Tennessee high school who posted a video to the school's You-Tube channel. In the video the assistant principal explains the school's new, stricter dress code that prohibits all students—girls and boys—from wearing revealing clothing, including athletic shorts. In the video the assistant principal says, "I know, boys, you're thinking, 'I don't understand why. It's not fair. . . .'" Then he leans in closer to the camera and says, "If you really want someone to blame, blame the girls, because they pretty much ruin everything. They ruin the dress code, they ruin, well, ask Adam. Look at Eve. That's really all you gotta get to, OK? You can go back to the beginning of time."

He ends with an aside to the boys, saying, "It'll be like that the rest of your life. Get used to it."

After the video went viral, the assistant principal insisted he had been kidding. The school put him on temporary leave and deleted the video, but the *Chattanooga Free Times Press* obtained a copy. I watched it. Several times. It confirms what I know to be true—that we are still under the sway of antiquated myths and misguided interpretations of religious parables. You may think these stories are the stuff of "once upon a time" and have nothing to do with you or your times. But "once upon a time" is now, because the past is laced into the present on the needle and thread of stories. Solid things come and go, but stories endure. They outlive the people who tell them; they jump from one continent to another; they continue to mold cultures for generations.

Why do the stories endure? Why did humans tell them in the first place? For a very simple reason: Life is hard. It's confusing. We have enough intelligence to ponder existence, but not enough to really understand what's going on here in our small corner of the vast universe. That's why we tell the stories. To ease the anxiety of being soft-skinned mortals. To inspire the soul to fathom eternity. To give order to what feels out of control. To guide, to blame, to warn, to shame. To make some kind of sense out of why people do what they do, why things happen the way they happen, and how we might all meet each other and daily life with less turmoil and more stability. That's why we cling to the old stories. That's how an assistant principle in Tennessee in the twenty-first century can reach back to a parable from 1500 BCE to wrap a complex conundrum in a simplistic explanation, to affix blame to one group of people in order to solve a problem for another group. In this case, blaming girls for how their exposed bodies affect boys, while letting boys off the hook for their own sexual urges and conduct. "If you really want someone to blame," he said, "blame the girls, because they pretty much ruin everything. . . . You can go back to the beginning of time."

Once metabolized, the old stories are hard to shake from the mind of an individual or the hierarchy of a family or the guiding principles of a country. Sometimes they are experienced as benign entertainment, and sometimes they are used, as the Tennessee assistant principal did, to remind women of the blame and shame we inherited from our founding Western mothers, starting with Eve, and followed by a long line of disgraced leading ladies.

It's important to know these stories and to ask questions like: Who told them? Why? And how have they maintained their authority all these years later? It's important to understand that the stories were not created to help women respect their bodies, intelligence, and legitimacy. They were not told to help women tap into their strength, or to use their voice to influence priorities at home and at work and in the world. Quite the opposite. They were told and are still told to bury the truth of our equality, values, and voice.

Becoming familiar with our culture's origin stories and tracing their influence is a surprisingly effective way to take stock of our own lives and to claim an authentically powerful voice—one that proclaims not only our equal rights but also our unique capacities and concerns. By "origin stories," I am referring to stories from modern Western cultures, including Adam and Eve from the Old Testament, Pandora and Cassandra from Greek myths, and novels and plays from the canon of Western literature.

Remember that many of the creation myths from our earlier ancestors—the indigenous, pre-colonized peoples from cultures around the world—painted a different picture of the origin of women and men, and their worth and roles. In many of those stories, neither sex was created to dominate the other. Both men and women shared the responsibility to help the community survive, thrive, and connect with the sacred. Researching and reading these stories has given me a different vision of "human nature" and what is possible. But they are not the stories that are driving our culture today; they are not the stories most of us were raised on.

When I began to pay attention to our origin tales, I suddenly felt their tentacles everywhere. It was as if I was hearing voices from across the ages—the specific voices of the men and the missing voices of the women. So many of the stories impart the same themes: men are the morally pure and noble ones; women are the ones who succumb to evil and tempt the men. The old stories paint a wildly improbable description of what it means to be a woman: erotically seductive yet emotionally fickle, in need of protection yet dangerous, all at the same time. Who could trust such a creature?

And so, I am calling those old storylines into question.

We'll start with the story of the first woman.

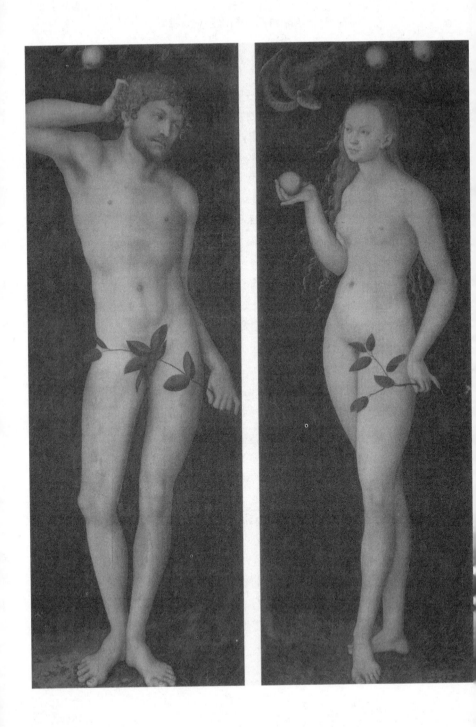

EVE

And the woman said unto the serpent,

We may eat of the fruit of the trees of the garden:

But of the fruit of the tree which is in the
midst of the garden, God hath said,

Ye shall not eat of it, neither shall
ye touch it, lest ye die.

And the serpent said unto the woman,
Ye shall not surely die:

For God doth know that in the day ye eat thereof,

then your eyes shall be opened, and ye shall
be as gods, knowing good and evil.

And when the woman saw that
the tree was good for food,

and that it was pleasant to the eyes, and
a tree to be desired to make one wise,

she took of the fruit thereof, and did eat,

and gave also unto her husband
with her; and he did eat.

—GENESIS 3:5

I'm not much of a museumgoer. I don't have an eye for modern art, and my knowledge of classic art is slim. So when a painting grabs my heart, it joins a small family of favorites. There's a painting of Joan of Arc by Jules Bastien-Lepage that hangs in the Metropolitan Museum of Art. Every now and then, when I'm in New York City, I like to drop in on that painting, as if it were a distant relative I enjoy seeing from time to time. It's huge, covering almost an entire wall. Joan is in a garden. She looks skyward, her eyes the color of a blue flame. In the background are diaphanous wisps of angels and other mysterious figures. If I have time, I sit on a bench directly in front of the painting, in silent conversation with Joan and her ethereal companions. There is something about that garden, and the thin veil between Earth and heaven, that gives me pause, and rest, and a sense that beyond this world of confusion and conflict, vibrating at a frequency we humans rarely perceive, is a different reality, something both mysterious and familiar, a Garden of Eden where our better angels prevail.

There is another painting, in another museum, that has also become a touchstone for me—*Adam and Eve*, created in 1528 by a German painter with a fantastical name: Lucas Cranach the Elder. It was this painting that led me to the Old Testament creation story found in the book of Genesis in the Bible. Of course, I knew the story before I ever set eyes on the painting. Even those not raised in a religious home, or those who grew up in other traditions, know the characters: Adam, the first human, the first man, made in God's perfect image; Eve, the second human, the woman, created from the body of the man to be his helpmate.

The moral of the story is open for interpretation, depending on the translation you read, or the scholars you trust, or the religious tradition in which you may have been brought up. But the basic plot goes like this: After creating Adam and Eve, God the Father (there's no mother) places them in the Garden of Eden—naked, safe, and well provided for. They know nothing of suffering, need, or conflict. They are immortal, innocent, garden-dwelling creatures. God gives Adam and Eve only one rule: not to eat the fruit from the tree of knowledge of good and evil, lest they shall die. Then a snake tempts Eve, saying, "Ye shall not surely die." In fact, says the snake, the fruit will open your eyes and make you wise. Eve listens to the snake, but not only that, she listens to herself: "And when the woman saw that the tree was good for food, and that it was pleasant to the eyes, and a tree to be desired to make one wise, she took of the fruit thereof, and did eat, and gave also unto her husband with her; and he did eat."

As punishment for Eve's disobedience and for Adam's succumbing to his wife's temptation, God curses them. He curses the woman with painful childbirth and subservience to her husband. He curses the husband with constant toil. He curses both of them with illness, old age, and death, and he exiles them from the Garden of Eden. Everything after that goes downhill. All because of Eve's curiosity and defiance, and Adam's submission to Eve's sin. *The Fall*.

I have visited *Adam and Eve* by Lucas Cranach the Elder only once, when I was newly divorced and still reeling from my own fall. I had followed my instincts and traded the safety of the known for the desire "to be made wise." I had gone against the gods of my culture: parents, husband, marriage, tradition. Even though my marriage had failed because of decisions made by and behaviors taken by both my husband and myself, it felt as though there was a scarlet letter on my chest—that I had sinned, that I had failed, that I had shamefully left the Garden.

That was the state of mind I was in when I viewed the Cranach painting in the Uffizi Gallery in Florence, Italy. As I stood before the images of Eve and Adam, I felt a kinship with their story for the first time in my life. All of the guilt and shame I was feeling, as well as the freedom and the power, were there in Eve's face. On Adam's face I read the story of men's inherited and often unconscious belief in their superiority and therefore their right—their role—to dominate. I was so struck by the painting that I made it my screen saver, since unlike Joan of Arc, I would not be able to visit Adam and Eve on a regular basis.

I never grow tired of staring at the Cranach painting. It's actually two paintings—two large panels linked together. In one, Eve stands against a blue-black background. In her left hand she holds a small branch, its green leaves barely covering her vulva. In her right hand she holds a red apple—"The fruit of the tree which is in the midst of the garden." You can see her teeth marks in the apple's flesh. Behind Eve, emerging from the darkness, a serpent has coiled itself around a branch, aiming its head like an arrow directly at her.

In the other panel, Adam stands against a similar dark background. He, too, holds a leafy branch in one hand to cover his genitals. With his other hand, he scratches the top of his head, as if to say, "I don't know what's going on here. Don't look at me." He blends into the dark background and has a drowsy, self-satisfied look on his face. In contrast, Eve seems lit from within. Her eyes are piercing; her mouth turns upward in a slight smile. Depending on how you relate to the story, you might say that Eve has the look of a temptress—shrewd and cunning, as if shot through with the snake's venom, deserving of the reputation that will haunt her through the ages: "Second in creation, first to sin." You might say that if it were not for Eve's transgression, humankind would still be abiding in the uncorrupted Garden of Eden.

Or, if you relate to the story as I do, you would say something else. You would say that Eve looks awake—curious about everything, at home in her body, and in vibrant communion with nature. She also looks fed up with Adam's attitude of lazy, firstborn entitlement. She hands the apple to Adam because she knows they cannot stay in the garden of innocence forever, that she and Adam will need to grow up, to take care of themselves, to take responsibility. She accepts direction from the snake, who in biblical times was a symbol of wisdom—the one who sheds the skin of ignorance and is born again. "And the serpent said unto the woman, Ye shall not surely die: For God doth know that in the day ye eat thereof, then your eyes shall be opened, and ye shall be as gods, knowing good and evil." Like the mythic Phoenix bird, the snake understands that the death God spoke of was not literal death, but rather the death of the child-self, the unconscious self, the fearful self who chooses the safe status quo and therefore never fulfills his or her God-given potential.

The way I see it, Eve is humankind's first grown-up. The "temptation" she succumbs to is the most fundamental human yearning—to know oneself, to find one's own path, and to courageously engage with the big world beyond the garden of childhood. To grow up is to admit that life is challenging and that we are responsible for our own behavior and for the well-being of one another. In psychological terms, the urge to grow up is called individuation, and in mythological terms it is called the hero's journey—the inner calling to push off from the shore of mother and father, to test limits, to know your worth, to speak your truth, to claim authentic selfhood.

Because the word *hero* has long been associated exclusively with the word *man*, women may not relate to the idea of being on a hero's journey. This is an understandable (yet erroneous) assumption. The Bible is full of heroic men celebrated for their hero's journeys—from Noah to Job, and from Moses to Jesus. Men whose stories map the arc of exile from family or homeland, of being tested, of losing faith and regaining it. Men who learn about goodness and evil through the fire of their own experiences. Only Eve has been demonized for answering the same call. While the men of the Bible are allowed to fall in their humanness and rise in wisdom, Eve only falls. And womankind bears the scars of her sin instead of the honor of her courage.

In the classic book *The Power of Myth*, the venerated scholar Joseph Campbell and the journalist Bill Moyers have an extended conversation about origin stories from many traditions. In one chapter, Moyers asks Campbell: "Does the idea of woman as sinner appear in other mythologies?"

Campbell answers: "No, I don't know of it elsewhere. The closest thing to it would be perhaps Pandora with Pandora's box, but that's not sin, that's just trouble. The idea in the biblical tradition of the Fall is that nature as we know it is corrupt, sex in itself is corrupt, and the female as the epitome of sex is a corrupter. Why was the knowledge of good and evil forbidden to Adam and Eve? Without that knowledge, we'd all be a bunch of babies still in Eden, without any participation in life. Woman brings life into the world. Eve is the mother of this temporal world. Formerly you had a dreamtime paradise there in the Garden of Eden—no time, no birth, no death—no life."

Many scholars have gone back into the earliest translations of the book of Genesis and noted that in the original Hebrew text "the knowledge of good and evil" meant the knowledge of how things really work for human beings, here in the realm of time and birth and death. To be human often feels as if we arrived here without an instruction book, longing for direction, aware of our better angels and, at the same time, vulnerable to our own ignorance and fear and greed. Isn't this the crux of human life and the lesson of every great teaching tale? That we are lost, but we can be found. That we suffer, but we can grow wise. That if we take personal responsibility, we might grasp the "knowledge of good and evil" and chart a noble path home.

But taking responsibility so as to grow wise is often not our first response to suffering. A more common, knee-jerk reaction is to look for someone else to blame . . . blame your partner for the problems in the marriage, blame your boss for the problems at work, blame a group of people—from a different race, religion, nationality—for the problems in the world. Blame the snake! Blame Eve for her wanton and witchy ways. Blame Adam for being a cuckold, a sissy, an emasculated snowflake. Blame God, as Adam did, for making the woman in the first place.

But in truth, there is no one to blame for the conundrum in which we find ourselves. Life is full of challenges, humans are full of desires, and each one of us is faced with daily choices between good and evil. We long for Eden—that state of being where the opposites are united, where peaceful abiding is the norm. But what if the whole point of life is to find Eden within and, in doing so, to create heaven on Earth? This is what the awareness of good and evil really means: to recognize that all the light and all the darkness in the world also dwells within your own heart, and instead of blaming the "other," our task is to become like gods—self-aware and responsible for choosing goodness over evil.

This is what Eve did. She woke up; she grew up. I think of the story of Adam and Eve as a classic hero's journey tale— the leave-taking of childlike consciousness and the journey toward mature self-responsibility. But somewhere along the way in the storytelling, blame set in. Someone had to take the blame for why life was so difficult and humans so vulnerable. Cue: the Fall.

It's important to understand the significance of how our society's origin story is based in blame. It's good to contemplate what our culture would be like if the first woman had not been branded as "second born, first to sin." How would things be different if humankind's first big mistake wasn't to follow the lead of the woman? And if Eve's punishment hadn't been subservience to Adam? I am reminded of those questions every morning when I turn on my computer and look at the screen saver. Before I get to work, I say hello to the exiles, Adam and Eve, and I say a little prayer for all of us. That we become less blameful of others and more responsible for ourselves, for each other, for the Eden we must protect. That we become less like lost children and more like wise seekers. Then, as T. S. Eliot says, "The end of all our exploring will be to arrive where we started and know the place for the first time."

PANDORA

Both Eve and Pandora bring death into the world.
This is a curious reversal of the fact
that women bring life into the world,
but it says something about the
meaning of "woman"
within a religion dominated by male gods.

—POLLY YOUNG-EISENDRATH

Here's another origin story, brought to us by the ancient Greeks, or, to be more precise, by the poet Hesiod.

Zeus, the king of the gods, gave the god Prometheus the task of creating the first men. Prometheus fashioned them out of clay, making an all-male society of immortal humans who worshipped and served the gods and ate freely from splendid gardens. Prometheus grew to love his creations. Without getting Zeus's permission, he fed the humans the gods' sacred meat and stole for them fire from heaven, giving the men godlike power. This enraged Zeus, who, in retaliation, chained Prometheus to a rock and sent a giant eagle to peck at his liver. To mankind he sent a different punishment: woman.

In Hesiod's words, Zeus said to Prometheus: "You stole the fire and outwitted my thinking; but it will be a great sorrow to you, and to men who come after. As the price of fire, I will give them an evil, and all men shall fondle this, their evil, close to their hearts, and take delight in it." This evil was none other than Pandora, the first woman. The gods and goddesses on Mount Olympus each contributed to Pandora's creation by giving her gifts. Zeus gave her a "foolish and idle nature," writes Hesiod. From the goddess Aphrodite, Pandora received her seductive beauty—a "beautiful evil . . . not to be withstood by men." The god Hermes gave her "a shameful mind and deceitful nature" as well as the tendency to speak "lies and crafty words." And last but not least, the goddess Hera gave Pandora the most dangerous gift of all, a "woman's curiosity."

Hesiod writes, "From her is the race of women and female kind: of her is the deadly race and tribe of women who live amongst mortal men to their great trouble, no helpmeets in hateful poverty, but only in wealth. And as in thatched hives bees feed the drones whose nature is to do mischief—by day and throughout the day until the sun goes down the bees are busy and lay the white combs, while the drones stay at home in the covered hives and reap the toil of others into their own bellies—even so Zeus who thunders on high made women to be an evil to mortal men, with a nature to do evil."

Zeus sent Pandora down to Earth and married her off to Prometheus's brother. As a wedding gift, Zeus gave Pandora a large storage jar (mistranslated into English as a box) with the explicit warning that she must never open it. But after a while that gift of curiosity got the better of her, and Pandora lifted the lid. Suddenly, there was a hissing sound and a horrible odor. Terrified, she slammed the lid down, but it was too late. Zeus had trapped in the jar the spirit of every kind of suffering that if released would plague mankind forever: toil, sickness, famine, jealousy, hatred, war, and the cycle of birth and death. And because of Pandora and her "nature to do evil," those spirits were now alive in the world, and suffering was humankind's fate.

At least that's how Hesiod told it. Hesiod lived in the eighth century BCE, around the same time as the epic poet Homer, author of the *Odyssey* and the *Iliad*. Historians refer to Hesiod's poems as the "Genesis" of Greek mythology. Like Genesis in the Bible, Hesiod's versions of ancient Greek myths still affect our modern consciousness. We may have only the foggiest memory of the Greek gods and warriors (maybe from a sixth-grade social studies project, or a comic book, or in my case from the stories my mother read aloud at bedtime from Edith Hamilton's *Mythology: Timeless Tales of Gods and Heroes*). But the names and the feats of those mythological figures are all around us, in our language and art and philosophies, and above us, in the stars where the constellations bear their names.

After my mother died my sisters and I divided up her most cherished belongings. My first choice was a collection of my mother's favorite books, including her small and tattered paperback edition of Hamilton's *Mythology*. I took that book down recently and reread some of those stories that my mother seemed to love, even though they read like violent, misogynistic soap operas. My mother explained away the violence and misogyny in all kinds of literature by telling us that humans are a bickering species, that men are babies (and yet, she always added, they still they rule the world), and this has been so from the beginning of time.

Actually, "the beginning of time" is a misnomer, at least in the way time is measured in the history books most of us read. History is generally referred to as the time period after the invention of writing. The first written records date back to 3200 BCE, in Egypt, and therefore, history is said to "begin" about five thousand years ago. But anatomically modern humans have been around for two hundred thousand plus years. The planet itself is 4.5 billion years old.

Imagine how many stories are hiding under the cover of prehistory, and how many lifestyles, organizing principles, and value systems have come and gone since the real beginning of time. Just because the written word is currently the most dependable record of the stories our ancestors told doesn't mean there aren't other stories. Archaeologists, paleontologists, and anthropologists have been studying prehistoric cultures and peoples, trying to piece together not only stories we have never heard but also the ways in which the scribes of history have rewritten reality to fit into their prevailing worldviews. The noted historian Sally Roesch Wagner says, "History isn't what happened. It's who tells the story." Her research into women's history, and stretching back further into women's prehistory, reveals glaring evidence of the ways in which stories change according to who tells them. We may think of history as "fact," as if some ancient omniscient scribe, untainted by a biased viewpoint or a selective memory, had told the whole story. But just like now (think cable news shows, think about the people with the loudest Twitter fingers or the most compelling Instagram feeds), those who tell the tales are human beings with all sorts of motivations, including strong opinions, an ax to grind, an ego to stoke, a system to uphold.

We relate to Hesiod's words as if they flowed directly from the mouths of the gods, but Hesiod interpreted old myths and folk tales from the oral tradition, changing many of them to reflect the issues of his times and to protect the privilege of the ruling, patriarchal class. Marguerite Johnson, a British professor of ancient history and classical languages, sums up the trail left from Hesiod's version of the Pandora myth like this: "[It] tells the tale of the fall from innocence, the hardships of mortal existence, and the fear of women. . . . Pandora was a trap—gorgeous on the outside, and evil on the inside—and she marked the end of paradise."

Sound familiar? Like Eve, Pandora left her stamp on womanhood: impulsive, untrustworthy, and disobedient. And like Eve, she released evil and suffering into a previously male paradise. Hesiod's storytelling is yet another smear tactic against females—woman as scapegoat, someone to blame for the very fact that life is difficult, that troubles are common, that illness and death befall each of us. The Jungian writer Polly Young-Eisendrath writes, "Exactly like Eve in the Garden of Eden, this Greek first woman is both the first female mortal and the instigator of mortality in the human race. To be mortal means to die, and both Eve and Pandora bring death into the world. This is a curious reversal of the fact that women bring life into the world, but it says something about the meaning of 'woman' within a religion dominated by male gods."

In versions that predate Hesiod's storytelling, Pandora was not a punishment at all but rather a gift. In fact, the name Pandora means "all-giving." Earlier versions of the spoken myth, pieced together from the artwork on fifth century BCE pottery, paint Pandora as an embodiment of the fertility of the earth, a healer and life giver. Even in Hesiod's telling, the Pandora myth ends on a surprising note, a spillover perhaps from the original spoken versions, and one that holds out a smidgen of redemption for womankind. When Pandora realized what she had let loose upon the world, Hesiod writes, she quickly shut the lid of the jar, just in time to trap the last of the spirits inside. Her name was Elpis—the spirit of hope. "Only Hope was left within her unbreakable house," writes Hesiod. "Hope remained under the lip of the jar, and did not fly away."

Some mythologists say that when Pandora realized what she had done, she enticed Elpis to stay with the humans, to give them the strength to deal with her mistake. Others say it was not Pandora who released the evil curses at all; rather, she was the one who discovered the opened jar and she held back Elpis—Hope—to help humans withstand the trials of mortal existence. It's time to lead with the ending of the story—to highlight the part where Pandora holds back Elpis as a gift to us struggling mortals. It's time to tell stories where no one is to blame for the human predicament and all of us are responsible for forging a hopeful path forward.

SHE'S GOT THE WHOLE WORLD IN HER HAND

Better is the wickedness of a man
than a woman who does good.

—FROM THE BOOK OF ECCLESIASTICUS

My parents were raised in religious homes, yet by the time they married both of them had rejected their faith with the kind of fervor that could only be called religious. They were adamantly, dogmatically anti-religion. Our home was a faith-free zone. Regarding the big life-and-death questions, there were no holy texts, no guidance, no answers—the lack of which seemed not to bother other family members. But I was the kind of kid who yearned for *something*, some answers to the vexing nature of being human.

As early as four or five I couldn't fall asleep at night, over-whelmed by the thought of death. In third grade when a class-mate died from childhood cancer, I raised my hand and tried to organize a discussion about it (foreshadowing my work as a conference convener), but the teacher—the formidable Miss

Gray—shut me down, saying that Jimmy had gone to heaven and that was all we needed to know. Yet I had heard at home that heaven was a figment of a fearful imagination, so I raised my hand again and asked Miss Gray, "Does heaven really exist?" I was sincere. Miss Gray was angry. At the end of the day she marched me to the principal's office, where we waited for my mother to arrive.

I remember this scene vividly—Miss Gray whispering with the school secretary as I sat on the bench outside the principal's door, my feet in their brown leather shoes dangling above the scuffed linoleum floor. When my mother showed up, the principal admonished her for raising her children in a godless home.

Indeed, there was no God in our home, but there *were* those stories about Greek gods and goddesses, and there were the words of the Psalms and the Sermon on the Mount (early literature, my mother explained), as well as a reverence for nature, beauty, and justice. But that wasn't enough for me. My girlhood rebellion took the form of going to Catholic mass with my best friend and listening to gospel music on my parents' record player. My favorite singer was Marian Anderson, who got the stamp of approval from my mother, not because of Anderson's piety but because she was a champion of civil rights.

The first record I ever bought was Marian Anderson's *Deep River*. I memorized songs from that album, songs like "Deep River," "Nobody Knows the Trouble I've Seen," and "He's Got the Whole World in His Hands." I loved the feeling in the melodies and the mystery of the words. I would sing "Deep

River" to myself in the dark when I couldn't fall asleep. I had no idea what the lyrics meant—"Deep river, Lord," Marian Anderson sang with longing rising up from her gut. "I want to cross over into campground." Campground? What campground? I imagined that all the lucky people who went to church knew what Miss Anderson was referring to. And the next lines: "Oh, don't you want to go to the Gospel feast? That Promised Land, where all is peace?" Yes, I did want to go! I wanted to go wherever Miss Anderson was singing about; I wanted to go there the way other kids my age wanted to go to a dance or a football game.

Other lyrics puzzled me, too, especially the ones that described God as a father, as a man. "He's got the whole world in His hands," Marian Anderson sang. "He's got you and me, sister, in His hands." That's the line that got my sisters and mother laughing when I would sing along to the record. But I took the words seriously and literally. I asked my mother why in that song, and in the Old Testament Psalms she read to us, was God a man? It seemed preposterous to me that an entity capable of birthing the universe would be male, or even have a gender at all.

"Don't you think God would be female since we're the ones who give birth?" I asked my mother.

My mother answered with the same dismissive tone she used for any questions about religion: "God has no gender," she said, "because there is no God."

When I got to Barnard College in the 1970s, one of the first classes I signed up for was the History of World Religions, given in a large lecture hall across the street from Barnard at

Columbia University. It was an interesting time and place to be studying ancient religious texts. Columbia had been a hotbed of revolutionary fervor that had left in its wake a distrust of the classics. My crusty old professor was out of his element with this new batch of students who questioned everything from hierarchical structures to the pronouns used in prayers.

I recently found my final paper from that class. It was in a box of letters and drawings and schoolwork that my mother had saved, my papers from Barnard separated from the rest, preserved in a plastic bag. My mother was a proud Barnard graduate. She was dismayed when I quit her alma mater after my sophomore year and followed an Eastern guru to California. I don't know what my mother found more appalling—that I was a college dropout or that a daughter of hers would even utter the word *guru* with a straight face.

The term paper was about the *Book of Sirach*, also known as *Ecclesiasticus*, a book of moral instructions, some of which were discovered with the Dead Sea Scrolls. It was written by Ben Sirach, a Hebrew scholar who lived in Jerusalem around 200 BCE. My paper focused on two chapters in the book—"On Wives and Women" and "A Father's Care for His Daughter." At the top of my paper is a quote from Ben Sirach: "Better is the wickedness of a man than a woman who does good." I wonder if as a college freshman I found that line as shocking—and as illuminating—as I do now. *Better is the wickedness of a man than a woman who does good*. Now that says it all, as do some of the other lines I quoted from the *Book of Sirach*, like this one from the chapter "A Father's Care for His Daughter":

Keep strict watch over a headstrong daughter,
    or else, when she finds liberty, she will make use of it.
As a thirsty traveler opens his mouth
    and drinks from any water near him,
so she will sit in front of every tent peg
    and open her quiver to the arrow.

And this stanza that counsels men to keep young women away from older women, lest they be influenced by their "wickedness":

Do not let her reveal her beauty to any male, or spend
    her time with married women;
For just as moths come from garments, so a woman's
    wickedness comes from a woman.
Better a man's harshness than a woman's indulgence, a
    frightened daughter than any disgrace.

Using the language of the times, I ended my paper by calling Ben Sirach "male chauvinist pig number one." In the margins, my professor wrote, "Are you sure you aren't applying twentieth-century standards to a patriarchal value system that was normal then but no longer informs the ethos of our society?"

"Ha!" That's what I would say now to my Columbia professor. But at nineteen I did what girls and women have done since Ben Sirach's time. I chaffed against the messages in *Ecclesiasticus*, I complained about them in my paper, but I also internalized them. I took them in—into my self-image, into my behavior, into my body.

The essence of those teachings, many of which found their way into the Old and New Testaments of the Bible, can be distilled down to this:

1. Men are better than women, even the wicked men.
2. A woman's sense of shame is deserved. Shame for what? Our out-of-control emotions and our wanton sexuality that has the power to tempt a man and destroy his virtue.
3. A woman should be silent, with a "bound up mouth."
4. Men dominate women to protect women from other men.
5. Alliances between women are dangerous.

After finding the term paper in my mother's memorabilia, I went looking for the ways in which the themes and directives in *Ecclesiasticus* influenced early leaders of Jewish and Christian theologies, and then trickled down to subsequent generations. I read different translations of the Bible, as well as the ancient accounts of Jewish rabbis and the earliest Christian monks and nuns—the Desert Fathers and Mothers. I studied the words of Saint Paul, Saint Tertullian, and Saint Augustine, especially Augustine's analysis of Genesis in his book *Confessions*, where he puts forth his influential ideas that women are prone to heresy and their disobedience is at the foundation of all human sinfulness. I read a slew of more modern takes on Genesis, including academic interpretations and blogs and tweets from contemporary Bible literalists. And I explored the ways in which biblical themes show up in classical literature and modern media, from *Paradise Lost* to *The Scarlet Letter*, and from *Star Trek* to *Harry Potter*.

I share here but a few of the more salient quotations from some of Western religions' foundational thinkers and texts. If it seems as if I cherry-picked only the most incendiary and misogynistic excerpts, I invite you to read deeper into any of these books and authors. I am only scratching the surface here.

I'll start with this prayer, from the ancient siddur, recited still by Orthodox Jewish men each morning:

"Blessed are you, Lord our God, Ruler of the Universe, who has not made me a woman."

It was difficult for me to choose only a few quotes from the early Christian thinkers, monks, and saints. There are so many! Here's a small sampling:

From Timothy:

A woman should learn in quietness and full submission. I do not permit a woman to teach or to assume authority over a man; she must be quiet. For Adam was formed first, then Eve. And Adam was not the one deceived; it was the woman who was deceived and became a sinner. But women will be saved through childbearing—if they continue in faith, love and holiness with propriety.

From Saint Augustine:

Woman does not possess the image of God in herself but only when taken together with the male who is her head, so that the whole substance is one image. But when she is assigned the role as helpmate, a function that pertains to her alone, then she is not the image of God. But as far as the man is concerned, he is by himself alone the image of God. . . .

From Saint Tertullian:

In pain shall you bring forth children, woman, and you shall turn to your husband and he shall rule over you. And do you not know that you are Eve? God's sentence hangs still over all your sex and His punishment weighs down upon you. You are the devil's gateway; you are she who first violated the forbidden tree and broke the law of God. It was you who coaxed your way around him, whom the devil had not the force to attack. With what ease you shattered that image of God: Man! Because of the death you merited, even the Son of God had to die.

From Saint Clement of Alexandria:

[For women] the very consciousness of their own nature must evoke feelings of shame.

From Saint Thomas Aquinas:

As regards the individual nature, woman is defective and misbegotten, for the active force in the male seed tends to the production of a perfect likeness in the masculine sex; while the production of woman comes from a defect in the active force.

From Martin Luther:

If [women] become tired or even die, that does not matter. Let them die in childbirth, that is why they are there.

Ouch. But there's more! If things were as simple as "man, good/woman, bad," women might have risen up earlier and exposed the misogyny at the heart of our guiding moral doctrines. But even as the ancient Greeks and the Hebrew patriarchs and the Christian saints warned about women's primal wickedness, they also extolled the sacred wisdom at the core of femininity. Sure, there were Pandora and Eve and their tainted progeny down through the ages, but there were also other figures who represented the "divine feminine." The Greeks personified the divine feminine as Sophia—the bearer of wisdom. She can be found throughout the books of the Old Testament. Ben Sirach writes extensively of Sophia, whom he calls Lady Wisdom, and to whom he ascribes god-like status:

The word of God most high is the fountain of Wisdom;
And her ways are everlasting commandments.
To whom hath the root of Wisdom been revealed?
Or who hath known her wise counsels?

But still, he can't seem to help himself. His advice on how to plumb the depth of "her wise counsels" is almost laughable: "Happy is the person who meditates on Sophia," Sirach writes, "who reflects in one's heart on Sophia's ways and ponders her secrets, pursuing her like a hunter, and lying in wait on her paths."

This is the dangerous, crazy-making irony at the heart of so many of our traditions, where the archetype of "The Lady" is a holy counselor, but actual ladies are evil temptresses. Read the psalms and the prayers, listen to the mass, walk through any museum and behold woman portrayed as the Divine Feminine, the Holy Mother, and the Sovereign Queen of Heaven. You might get the wrong impression. You might think divine femininity had afforded women spiritual authority and personal autonomy, but let's be clear: while we are told that the male is made in God's perfect image, we are warned that the female is not inherently divine. She must work for it. If she remains quiet, virginal, and subservient, then maybe her sacred spark will burn brighter than her sinful instincts.

This age-old dualism—the worship of the divine feminine and yet the mistrust of flesh-and-blood women—confuses and silences women. It confuses and provokes men. And it leads us right up to today. Our culture still—either overtly or subtly—presents women with a choice: you can be a good girl (gentle,

submissive, pure), or you can be a bad girl (empowered, embodied, sexual). Of course, we know that most women have an interesting and ever-changing mixture of qualities brewing within them. We are not just a good girl or a bad girl. We are not only the Madonna or the whore, as the old trope goes. I revere the parts of myself that are classically depicted in those "Madonna" archetypes: the serene, the benevolent, the caregiving. Sometimes I activate those aspects of myself. It took me awhile (and lots of therapy) to own and love the "whore" archetype—my sensuality, my wildness, my erotic nature and sexual needs. I am all of the above. I am gentle and empowered. Serene and wild. Maternal and sexual. These are not good or bad dichotomies. They are qualities that make us human.

There's a statue of Sophia in the city of Sofia, Bulgaria. It was erected in 2000 to replace a statue of Lenin that had dominated the city for years. Standing tall—seventy-two feet above the central square—Sophia spreads her arms, embracing the city. An owl, depicting holy wisdom, perches on her shoulder. She wears a tight and diaphanous dress that reveals her breasts, and nipples, and the shape of her whole body. A golden crown—the symbol of power—sits on her head; in her hand she holds the wreath of peace. She is erotic and pagan, holy and on high. She is everywoman and she is queen. She stands in her body without it being a temptation, or a curse, or an offering to anyone. And she's got the whole world in her hand—a world of peace. May it be so.

LISTENING
TO CASSANDRA

The hardest times for me
were not when people challenged what I said,
but when my voice was not heard.

—CAROL GILLIGAN

I began the Introduction to this book with the Greek myth of
Cassandra because although her name may not be as notorious
as Eve's or Pandora's, her story resonates so clearly with our
times. She could foresee the future, yet her words fell flat. She
was disbelieved, disregarded, and gaslighted.

Gaslight is one of my favorite new verbs to enter the *Merriam-*
Webster Dictionary. The word also was one of the winners of
the American Dialect Society's 2016 Word of the Year. I like
the simplicity of their definition—"Gaslight: to psychologically manipulate a person into questioning their own sanity."
The word can be traced back to a 1938 play called *Gas Light*,
which was adapted into a popular and brilliant 1944 film by
the same name. I watched the movie recently. It stars Charles
Boyer and Ingrid Bergman and is about a husband hiding his
criminal intentions by manipulating his wife into thinking she

is losing her mind. He dims the gaslights in their house yet pretends nothing has changed. The floorboards creak as he rummages in the attic for stolen jewels, yet he claims his wife is hearing noises. He goads her into overwrought outbursts and warns he will commit her to an institution. (Spoiler alert: at the end of the film Bergman's character reverse-gaslights her husband by pretending that indeed she has lost her mind and therefore cannot help him when the police arrive to take him away.)

Cassandra's curse is an ancient example of gaslighting, and it is relived on a daily basis by women around the world: we know the truth of our own experiences, yet we are told we are lying or overreacting; we can see consequences on the horizon, but it's still "common knowledge" that women's emotions cloud their vision, that we tend toward hysteria—even madness—and therefore are not to be believed.

You can go all the way back to texts from ancient Egypt, Persia, and Greece for the earliest examples of gaslighting. The Greeks proposed that a large percentage of women had mental illness, and that their madness was derived from a refusal to honor the phallus, which caused an affliction they called uterine melancholy. The cure? The Persian physician Melampus wrote that "women should be treated with the herb hellebore, and then urged to join carnally with several strong men. Thus they will be healed and recover their wits." Melampus's contemporary, Hippocrates, the founder of Western medicine, first coined the term *hysteria* from *hystera*, Greek for uterus, believing that women's wombs moved throughout their bodies, inducing a "lack of control and extravagant feelings," what he called uterine fury.

Well, of course women were furious! You try being a woman in ancient Persia or Greece. Or later on in Victorian Europe and America, when male doctors tried to cure female hysteria by using an "electro-mechanical medical instrument" (aka vibrator) to induce "hysterical paroxysm" (aka orgasm). If that didn't work, doctors would apply high-pressure douches, all to rid the woman—and here I'm combining words from several medical texts from the early 1800s—of her "hysterical emotions, frustrated weeping, excessive (or lack of) sexual desire, excessive vaginal lubrication, general irritability, inability to conceive a child or fulfill proper mothering duties, and a tendency to cause trouble." In some cases, a woman demonstrating any of these symptoms might be forced to enter an insane asylum or to undergo surgical hysterectomy.

The American Psychiatric Association dropped the term *female hysteria* in 1950. It was replaced with the more Freudian term *hysterical neurosis*, which was not dropped from the *Diagnostic Manual for Mental Health* (*DSM*) until 1980. And even today, the theory of a pathological "uterine fury" follows us, demeans us, and causes us to doubt and silence ourselves. But I see changes afoot. I see bold women everywhere taking what used to be called a tendency to cause trouble and rebranding it as a tendency to speak up, to confront the gaslighting, and to make our culture more caring, communicative, and emotionally intelligent. "Far from women as a species being irrational, overemotional, hysterical, lunatic or morally weak," writes the Australian author Jane Caro, "what strikes me about women and their history is just how damn sane we have managed to stay."

I thought of this recently when I watched the televised trial of Dr. Larry Nassar, the doctor who sexually abused hundreds of female athletes under the guise of medical treatment. Most of the young women were gymnasts, including Olympic gold medalists Simone Biles and Aly Raisman. Some were runners, softball and soccer players, dancers, rowers, skaters. Some had been children—as young as six years old—when the abuse began; others were in their teens and older. For almost thirty years, Dr. Nassar perpetrated the same pattern of abuse, offering faux medical treatments, using his paternalistic power to molest and silence young women. And if his own behavior wasn't bad enough, the adults in the institutions that hired him—universities, training camps, USA Gymnastics, the US Olympic Committee, and even some parents—did not believe the girls and women. Year after year after year, they did not report the stories of abuse; they did not remove Larry Nassar; they took the word of a doctor over the word of their girls.

Finally, Dr. Nassar was brought to trial because many of his victims were brave enough to come forward; some of them had been sexually molested as recently as the previous year, and others were still profoundly affected years later by the double trauma of being assaulted and disbelieved. These girls are our Cassandras, I thought, as I watched the trial. They knew what had happened to them, and they saw what would happen to others if Dr. Nassar wasn't stopped. They had spoken the truth, but no one had believed them and no one had acted on their behalf. What was different about this story was what happened next.

The presiding judge in the case was Rosemarie Aquilina, an

unusual judge to say the least. Before she sentenced Dr. Nassar to up to 175 years behind bars (for criminal sexual abuse as well as child pornography charges for possession of at least thirty-seven thousand incriminating videos and images), she set a new precedent for a courtroom by allowing time for more than 150 women to deliver victim impact statements, televised for the whole world to witness. No longer alone in their truth telling, bolstered by strength in numbers, and treated with respectful listening, the young women spoke with so much legitimate fury that it felt to me as if generations of Cassandras were speaking through them and being vindicated.

Judge Aquilina listened to each young woman carefully, offering encouragement and comfort. Before she opened the floor, she noted that she was giving the women a chance to finally be heard since they had been ignored or doubted when they reported Dr. Nassar's abuse in the past. And explaining to Nassar why she was requiring him to listen to the women, she said, "Spending four or five days listening to them is minor, considering the hours of pleasure you've had at their expense, ruining their lives." What struck me most, what took my breath away, was the way the judge responded to many of the women, attempting to repair, right then and there, the wounding of disbelief.

Following Olympic gold medalist Aly Raisman's testimony, Aquilina told her: "I'm an adult. I'm listening. I'm sorry it took this long, but I assure you that all of the words that you and your sister-survivors have said and will say are being considered for sentencing." To another victim she said, "Push away those nightmares. He's gone. Your words replace what he's done to you." To one considering suicide, she counseled, "Only the defendant would be better off if you were not here. Please stay with us. Stay with your family. Your children need you."

In the safety and dignity of her courtroom, the girls and women told their truths. They addressed Larry Nassar, who sat in handcuffs, only a few feet away. Some cried, some yelled, some almost whispered as they spoke of his late-night knocks on their hotel doors at the Olympics; how he touched their breasts and penetrated their anuses and vaginas with his bare hands while they were facedown on exam-room tables; how they were only children, some of them nine, or twelve, or fifteen; how he ruined their careers, caused them suicidal thoughts, and put them and their families through anguish.

Gymnast Jordyn Wieber was part of the gold-medal winning team at the 2012 Summer Olympics. She was the first person to testify. She told how Dr. Nassar began grooming her for abuse when she was eight. "Nobody was protecting us from being taken advantage of," she said. "Nobody was ever concerned whether or not we were being sexually abused." Aly Raisman echoed her words: "Your abuse started thirty years ago," she said. "But that's just the first reported incident we know of. If over these many years, just one adult listened, and had the courage and character to act, this tragedy could have been avoided. . . . Neither USA Gymnastics nor the United States Olympic Committee have reached out to express sympathy or even offer support. Not even to ask, how did this happen? What do you think we can do to help?"

Amanda Thomashow, a college athlete, said, "I reported it. Michigan State University, the school I loved and trusted, had the audacity to tell me that I did not understand the difference between sexual assault and a medical procedure." Jamie Dantzscher, gymnast and Olympic medalist, said, "I was attacked on social media. . . . People didn't believe me, even people I thought were my friends. They called me a liar, a whore, and even accused me of making all of this up just to get attention."

Athlete after athlete stood and spoke. I heard in each of their speeches the outrage and tone of how I imagine Cassandra must have spoken after years of being doubted and belittled, even as her words were proven true—just as millions of women throughout time have been discredited, ignored, disrespected, and made to suffer for telling uncomfortable, inconvenient truths. But this time, under the words of pain, I could sense a new wind gathering strength. When Aly Raisman rose to speak, the wind blew through her words like a storm: "Over these thirty years when survivors came forward," she said, looking directly at Larry Nassar, "adult after adult, many in positions of authority, protected you, telling each survivor it was O.K., that you weren't abusing them. In fact, many adults had you convince the survivors that they were being dramatic or had been mistaken. This is like being violated all over again. . . . Imagine feeling like you have no power and no voice. Well, you know what, Larry? I have both power and voice, and I am only beginning to use them. All these brave women have power, and we will use our voices."

On the last day of the trial Judge Aquilina read aloud the letter Larry Nassar had sent to her the night before, blaming the girls for being two-faced and vengeful. In the letter he trotted out a famous proverb from English literature, directing it toward his accusers: "Hell hath no fury like a woman scorned," he quoted. Those words made the courtroom gasp when the judge read them, but I wasn't surprised. I had been steeping myself in responses like Nassar's from every era and every corner of the world. I was glad he quoted those old words. We need to hear them in real time because only then do we understand the power they still wield. Only then will we replace them with our own words—words like the ones Judge Aquilina told the survivors at the end of the trial: "Leave your pain here," she said, "and go out and do your magnificent things."

THE SPELL
OF GALATEA

People who are placed on a pedestal
are expected to pose, perfectly.
Then they get knocked off when they fuck it up.
I regularly fuck it up.
Consider me already knocked off.

—ROXANE GAY

In Greek and Roman mythology, Venus (whom the Greeks called Aphrodite) was the goddess of love, beauty, pleasure, and procreation. But she was also a wrathful, vengeance-seeking goddess. She was particularly jealous of her sister goddesses and mortal women. There are many stories of Venus fighting with other females. Perhaps the men who came up with the ancient Greek and Roman storylines had the same twisted fascination with a "catfight" as many men do now.

Laced through the old myths is the dubious notion that women do not like or trust other women, that they rarely support one another, and that they are in perpetual competition for the attention and approval of men. This has not been my overriding experience with my sisters, my friends, or my colleagues. Certainly, there can be conflict and competition between women; there is conflict and competition between humans of all stripes. There is a whole lot of it between men. But when men compete, there's an aura of respectability, sportsmanship, the whole "band of brothers" trope. Even on the literal battlefield, even among adversaries, the noble warriors admire one another's spirit. But when women are in conflict, the stereotype is far from the noble warrior. Rather, it's mean girls, bitches, backbiters, Queen Bees. When women compete, when we try to outpace someone else (each other or, God forbid, a man), words like *ambitious* and *assertive* take on negative, accusatory tones.

In his narrative poem *Metamorphoses*, the Roman poet Ovid tells the tale of Pygmalion and Galatea, which begins with an example of Venus's wrath and her punishing spirit toward noncompliant females. When a group of women from the island of Cyprus fails to worship her properly, Venus turns them into prostitutes (which only confirms for me that the story was cooked up by a man). Ovid writes:

> For this, because of her divine anger,
>   they are said to have been the first to prostitute their
>   bodies
> and their reputations in public, and, losing all sense of
>   shame,
> they lost the power to blush, as the blood hardened in
>   their cheeks.

After Venus's curse has taken effect, and the prostitutes walk the streets, a famous Cyprian sculptor named Pygmalion shuns all women. He is disgusted not only by the whores of his city but also by the "wicked" sexuality of women in general. He retreats to his workshop and carves a statue out of ivory—a beautiful, white, chaste girl who has none of the defects of flesh-and-blood women.

Pygmalion having been affected by their wickedness,
which nature has given the feminine mind, celibate he
  lived
for many years without a partner of the couch.
In the meantime he sculpted white ivory happily
with wonderous art and wonderous skill, and gave it
  form,
with which no woman is able to be born,
and he fell in love with his own work.

The longer Pygmalion chisels, the more perfect his creation becomes in his eyes, until her beauty outshines any woman who has ever lived. And finally, when the statue is finished, he is smitten. He who scorned all real women finally has formed an image worthy of his gaze.

He kisses it and thinks his kisses are returned;
and speaks to it; and holds it,
and imagines that his fingers press into the limbs,
and is afraid lest bruises appear from the pressure.

He gives his statue a name—Galatea, which means "she who is milk white." He brings her gifts, professes his love, stretches her out on his couch, and embraces her. He drapes her in fine fabrics, adorns her with jewels on her fingers, in her ears, around her neck. So in love is Pygmalion with his creation that he ardently prays to Venus to make his statue real so he might marry her. Flattered by his worship, and moved by his longing for a virtuous woman, Venus brings Galatea to life. And Pygmalion loses no time. . . .

> Now real, true to life—
> the maiden felt the kisses given to her,
> and blushing, lifted up her timid eyes,
>   so that she saw the light and sky above,
>   as well as her rapt lover while he leaned
> gazing beside her—and all this at once—
> the goddess graced the marriage she had willed,
> and when nine times a crescent moon had changed,
> increasing to the full, the statue-bride
> gave birth. . . .

The myth of Pygmalion and Galatea has been painted by artists and interpreted by authors throughout the ages. Modern versions of the myth abound—in plays and films, and on TV and social media. Consider the disheveled, low-class Eliza Doolittle in *My Fair Lady*, transformed in speech, dress, and demeanor by Professor Henry Higgins. Only after the hard work of transforming her into a "lady" does the professor find her worthy of his love. Then there's the poor prostitute,

Vivian Ward, in the film *Pretty Woman*, who is fashioned into a new and improved (and marriage-worthy) version of herself by the wealthy businessman Edward Lewis. Countless other films, and books, and the spate of reality-TV makeover shows perpetuate the theme that the arbiter and molder of acceptable female beauty and behavior is men, or the marketplace, or the culture at large.

The theme doesn't repeat itself only in fictional Cinderella stories. Look around at real women; take an honest assessment of your own story. Why are we still preoccupied by an arbitrary notion of what makes a woman beautiful, sexually desirable, or worthy of love? Why do we sacrifice our comfort, time, money, authenticity, and even our health to live up to unattainable body images? Why do we curb our emotions, quiet our voices, restrict our ambition? Why the heck are we still under the spell of Galatea?

Asking those questions is the first step in breaking the spell. And the spell can be broken only by us—by women, together—because we, as much as anyone else, are buying into the myth. It is up to us to say no, we are not the daughters of "milk-white" Galatea, chiseled from ivory for the male gaze. Whether we are young women, struggling with issues of beauty and sexual attraction, or older ones, obsessed with staying thin and looking young, we are the ones with the power to awaken from the trance, to take back our bodies, our skin tone, our features, our hair and height and weight, and to love ourselves as we are.

This is not an easy task. It's not easy for young women, middle-aged women, old women. It's particularly difficult for women whose ethnicity, race, size, and sexuality brand them as "other." The physical archetype of Galatea is everywhere, from images that flood magazines and media of all kinds, to mannequins in stores, and to fashion models so young and pale and skinny that their health is at risk. The woman on the pedestal looks nothing like most of us. If we continue to compare ourselves to that image, we live in a prison of our own obsession with thinness, tightness, whiteness, and eternal girlishness. Some of us starve ourselves in order to be thin, or we hate ourselves when we aren't. Or we inject a poison to tighten or lighten the skin or go under the knife to alter the contours of our precious faces and the curvature of our natural shapes. Women of all ages and races and walks of life wear clothes that constrict our breath like corseted women from the Victorian age and shoes that hobble us as if we are ancient Chinese girls with bound feet.

Here's an interesting history lesson: Chinese foot binding began in the seventh century and was outlawed only in the early 1900s. The process of modifying a woman's foot to make it about three inches long was an excruciatingly painful ordeal. Called lotus feet, bound feet were considered erotic to Chinese men, as was the tottering, helpless gait of the women who underwent the disabling process. In the nineteenth century alone, an estimated 2 billion women had their feet bound. We look back at such mutilation and subjugation with horror, but how far have we really come? Don't the contemporary standards of beauty and sexiness still hurt women? I ended up wrecking my knees and needing surgery from years of walking on concrete sidewalks in boots with three-inch heels. Why did I do this? Why do we still do things that injure and betray our bodies?

It's one thing to take care of ourselves through healthy eating habits and exercise, to enjoy wearing beautiful clothes and fashioning our hair and adorning ourselves in ways that make us feel lovely or sexy or powerful—or however we want to feel. I am all for that. But it's another thing to be enslaved by a cultural fantasy of what a woman should look like, speak like, be like.

As a former midwife, a conference convener, and a writer, I have spent my career researching how women might free their psychological and physical well-being from the spell of Galatea. Never one just to learn *about* things, I have also tried a whole lot of healing therapies in my own life. Many have been helpful, but what I have taken away from all of them, and what is most worth sharing, is what I call "the first law of healing." Without this first step, real health and positive self-regard never run deep.

The first law of healing: *We want to care for the things we love.*

The first step in toppling Galatea from Pygmalion's pedestal is for you to love your own body just as it is now. To love *your* face, *your* skin, *your* shape, size, age. To love it first, and then to let your self-care arise naturally from the love and respect you have for who you are, not for who you should be in the eyes of others. *We want to care for the things we love.* Most of us have it backward: I'll love my body *if* it's thinner, if my thighs don't jiggle, if I change the way I look—my nose, my hair, my skin, my breasts, my neck, my belly. We diet or exercise or buy products in the hopes that maybe one day we will love what we see in the mirror. We regard the body as if it's a problem to be solved, as if there is something fundamentally wrong and it's up to us to bully ourselves into lovability. And because the motivation to care comes from the outside, from someone else's standard of acceptability, we cannot apply the first law of healing.

As long as we want to trade in the bodies we have for the perfect girl on her pedestal, we will not recover our true beauty and sense of worth. As long as we attach our sense of power and value to the way we are seen from the outside, we keep the spell of Galatea alive.

The current image of Galatea is a crazy-making one. It sends a mixed message of who we should look like and how we should act: we're supposed to have a small waist and a cute butt, wear push-up bras that create cleavage, totter around on heels that elongate and eroticize the leg, and do everything we can to eliminate the signs of aging. We're called a prude if we're not sexy enough and a slut if we take it too far. We're supposed to find that sweet spot between sensual and modest, approachable and restrained, vulnerable and feisty. It takes up so much of our time and creativity to play this game. Imagine if we stopped. Imagine putting more of your energy into being okay with who you are and less into hoping you look and act the part exactly how and when you are supposed to, worrying you never will, all while feeling fundamentally bad about your body type, facial features, skin tone, waist, butt, and boobs.

Maybe you are quite fine with how you look, but if so, you are part of an exclusive club. According to a research campaign called the Real Truth About Beauty: Revisited, sponsored by

Dove, only 4 percent of women around the world consider themselves beautiful, and anxiety about appearance begins at an early age. Ninety-two percent of teen girls would like to change something about the way they look, with body weight ranking the highest, and six out of ten girls are so concerned with the way they look that they actually opt out of participating fully in daily life—from going swimming and playing sports to visiting the doctor to going to school or even just to offering their opinions.

I am in my sixties, and Galatea continues to haunt me. I've come a long way, but I still can fall under her spell and crave a self that isn't mine—especially when it comes to my aging body. Recently I had surgery to remove a kidney stone. It took me many weeks to recover fully. For much of that time I had no appetite, and as a result I lost the ten pounds I am forever trying to lose. It was almost laughable the way the pain of the kidney stone became a pale memory compared to the pleasure of fitting into my old pants. This has happened to me so many times throughout my life that I came up with a name for it: the Trauma Diet. Whatever the appetite-eliminating trauma (heartbreak, illness, loss, anxiety), the result is always appreciated . . . thinness! Alas, before long, I'm back to my set point. You'd think by now I would understand that my particular body type is not made for size 6 pants, if what it takes to maintain that size is trauma.

I'm tired of being under the spell of Galatea. For me, awakening from the spell has a lot to do with letting go of my obsession with thinness and my resistance to aging, and, instead, loving the form I am lucky enough to inhabit, just as she is.

For other women, breaking the spell will be about losing other kinds of exhausting, self-negating feelings about their bodies and behavior. There are many ways to get off Galatea's pedestal, to reject the myth of the pale, chiseled, flawless female form and instead to be proud human women, uniquely ourselves, unashamed of our imperfections and idiosyncrasies. As the author Roxane Gay writes, "People who are placed on a pedestal are expected to pose, perfectly. Then they get knocked off when they fuck it up. I regularly fuck it up. Consider me already knocked off."

THE
GREATEST
BOOKS

Why do we think that stories by men
are deemed to be of universal importance,
and stories by women are thought
to be merely about women?

—JUDE KELLY

I grew up in a family of readers. Reading was our sport. Some of my most potent, full-bodied childhood memories involve reading: crying when Charlotte the spider saved Wilbur the pig; listening intently to my mother read aloud from Salinger's *Franny and Zooey* as my father drove on family trips; spending most of a summer vacation curled up on a porch swing, reading *Gone with the Wind* and *To Kill a Mockingbird*. For me, an excursion to the local library was a peak experience, the Olympics of reading. I can still picture the mossy, worn steps leading up to the old stone building where my mother would take her four little girls each week. I can smell the dusty air, see the muted light slanting through the narrow windows, and hear the sacred silence that was enforced by the solitary librarian, whose cat-eye reading glasses hung on a chain around her neck.

When the modern library was built downtown, things got even better. I received my own library card and was given free range within the fluorescent-lighted stacks. The aroma was crisp and papery—like a perpetual autumn day. I remember how independent I felt roaming the rows, running my hand along the books' spines, stopping at a compelling title. When I think back on the books I chose, it's like being given the results of a personality test: I checked out novels about human relationships, children and families, other cultures, and historical events. I read books by Laura Ingalls Wilder and Madeleine L'Engle. I read *The Secret Garden* and *Harriet the Spy* and *A Tree Grows in Brooklyn*. I was drawn to books about friendship and romance, love and loss, beauty and courage, grief and death. Books with rich language and relatable characters. Books that made me feel strong and seen. Books that made me feel less alone in my questions and fears.

In middle school I discovered Jane Austen and the Brontë sisters in my parents' shelves. Sometimes the books were over my head, but I enjoyed drowning in the adult world of complex relationships. I had no preconceived notions about what I should read, no opinions about what other people liked, and no shame about the types of books I loved. I never was interested in stories about conquest, war, sports, or heroic journeys. I had nothing against them but no chemistry with them.

Given that my mother was an English teacher and a literary snob, I am grateful to her for allowing me in those early years the freedom to develop my own bookish tastes. It wasn't until high school when I was put into an advanced English class that I encountered the concept of "literature." Apparently, smart people read the *Iliad* and the *Odyssey*. They admired books by Leo Tolstoy and Marcel Proust and Miguel de Cervantes; they memorized lines from *Hamlet* and *Moby-Dick*; they professed to love James Joyce's *Ulysses* (even though there's a good chance not one high school student ever understood what that book was all about).

What about the kinds of books I loved? The ones about intimate relationships, women's friendships, and emotional catharsis? Best not to mention those books in my honors English class. Even if they were beautifully written, they were chick lit; they were for girls. But I *was* a girl! And the male-dominated curriculum bored me. I read the books and I wrote the papers, but I felt little affinity with many of the characters or with the issues that motivated them. Vague questions arose in my consciousness about why I should care about a sailor obsessed with a white whale or a foolish man who attacked windmills and jousted with imaginary dragons. And why was Hamlet shamed for grieving the death of his father? Wouldn't grief be a better response than revenge? Or at least an equally interesting one? And if *Hamlet* was considered to be the greatest play in the Western canon, then why were there only two women in the cast: Hamlet's dishonored mother, Queen Gertrude, and Ophelia, his deranged girlfriend.

I remember bringing up in class the famous line that Hamlet says to his mother, "Frailty, thy name is woman," and questioning its legitimacy. My teacher—a short, ghostly pale, and pock-faced man whose incongruous name was Mr. King—explained away my concerns by saying wistfully that women were indeed frail in Shakespeare's day. "They still are frail," he said. "They just won't admit it. They pretend they can be as strong as men." I wanted to reply that Hamlet seemed like the frail one to me—afraid to say what he meant, to take a stand, to do *something* until it was too late. At least Ophelia did something, even if that something was to take her own life.

Later, when the class read *Anna Karenina*, I wanted to ask Mr. King why suicide seemed to be the only action available to women who found themselves in a difficult situation. The men in Tolstoy's tales went on exciting journeys or tested themselves in the public arena when the going got tough, while the women either stayed at home or killed themselves. But I was too intimidated by Mr. King and the intellectual kids in the "smart" class to voice my concerns. I figured I just wasn't sophisticated enough to appreciate real literature.

Eventually, I became choosier in what I read and what rang true about who I was, what I cared about, and how I might live my life. It took me a long time to gain trust in my own choices, to decide that, no, Hemmingway did *not* move me; war stories *were* horrendous; and it *did* matter that *Lolita* was a book about child abuse.

In college I was able to choose classes where we read books from other countries and cultures, and books by and about women. But still, the books by which all others were measured were the same books I had read in high school. Granted, things have changed since then. Through major effort, female authors and writers of color have been included in the curricula.

But search online for the "greatest books of all time" or "the best novels ever written" and check out contemporary lists. I collected and consolidated ten such lists (from universities and literary magazines and bookstores and libraries) and here are the results—the top fifteen best novels ever written:

1. *In Search of Lost Time* by Marcel Proust
2. *Don Quixote* by Miguel de Cervantes
3. *Ulysses* by James Joyce
4. *The Great Gatsby* by F. Scott Fitzgerald
5. *Moby-Dick* by Herman Melville
6. *Hamlet* by William Shakespeare
7. *War and Peace* by Leo Tolstoy
8. *The Odyssey* by Homer
9. *One Hundred Years of Solitude* by Gabriel García Márquez
10. *The Divine Comedy* by Dante Alighieri
11. *The Brothers Karamazov* by Fyodor Dostoyevsky
12. *Madame Bovary* by Gustave Flaubert
13. *The Adventures of Huckleberry Finn* by Mark Twain
14. *Lolita* by Vladimir Nabokov
15. *The Iliad* by Homer

And here is the list of the fifteen most-assigned books in American high schools today:

1. *Lord of the Flies* by William Golding
2. *The Great Gatsby* by F. Scott Fitzgerald
3. *1984* by George Orwell
4. *The Catcher in the Rye* by J. D. Salinger

5. *The Scarlet Letter* by Nathaniel Hawthorne
6. *To Kill a Mockingbird* by Harper Lee
7. *Animal Farm* by George Orwell
8. *Romeo and Juliet* by William Shakespeare
9. *Of Mice and Men* by John Steinbeck
10. *Hamlet* by William Shakespeare
11. *Wuthering Heights* by Emily Brontë
12. *Macbeth* by William Shakespeare
13. *Brave New World* by Aldous Huxley
14. *The Odyssey* by Homer
15. *The Adventures of Huckleberry Finn* by Mark Twain

These are the books from which young people learn what it means to be human, and yet the stories they tell are predominantly from the perspective of men, or at least a certain kind of man and his experiences, struggles, physicality, desires, and values. They are called the Great Books, whereas novels and memoirs that chart women's experiences, struggles, physicality, desires, and values are given their own category in bookstores—Women's Literature—as if a gender can be a genre. They are faulted for lacking "muscular prose" and for focusing too much on "relationships" (apparently a crime against literature).

I often hear women belittle themselves for reading books they consider to be "chick lit." But as fiction critic Jenny Geras asks, "Are there millions of clever men out there feeling guilty about reading John Grisham?" Or as bestselling fiction writer Jennifer Weiner says, "There's a certain dismissive tone that people can take when they're talking about memoirs by women.

When men tell a certain kind of story, everybody's like, 'Look how brave he's being.' When women talk about sex or miscarriage, it's like, 'Oh, exhibitionist! TMI over there. . . .' Want to make the world holler? Be female . . . then stand up and say, 'This thing that I created, this thing I made as a woman, for other women, is worth something.'"

If ever a "classic" novel by a woman makes it to the greatest-books-of-all-time lists, it is usually one by Virginia Woolf or George Eliot (who indeed was a woman writing under the pen name of a man to ensure that her works would be taken seriously). All praise to Woolf and Eliot—it took great courage for them writing in their times to find their authentic voice and style. The same goes for the Brontë sisters and Jane Austen, to name just a few, because, indeed, it is only those few who are remembered. Happily, women novelists began to show up on twentieth-century lists—writers like Harper Lee, Toni Morrison, Maya Angelou, and Isabel Allende. And women authors are proliferating magnificently in the twenty-first century; their books are beginning to appear on some of the more enlightened lists. (In Part III of this book, in the "Flip the Script" chapter, I offer ways for all of us to influence the creation of new lists.)

But still, an online search reveals that things haven't changed much in a couple of centuries. Critics often attribute this inequity to the historical lack of women writers. "What can we do?" they seem to be saying. "Women just weren't writing back then." We have to ask, Why? Why were there so few noted women writers over the centuries? Why do we still leave women out of the canon? Historians will point to the social norms of different eras that kept women in strictly enforced roles as mothers and caretakers of the family. They will explain that, compared to men, women were poorly educated and often illiterate. All true, but these are not the reasons that most intrigue me. I am more interested in the observation that Virginia Woolf made in 1929, in *A Room of One's Own*. In it she laments how over the ages, men have chosen which human values should prevail—elevating some and demeaning others, leading whole cultures to believe in the superiority of what Woolf called masculine values. For example, she writes: "Football and sport are considered important . . . or this is an important book, the critic assumes, because it deals with war. This is an insignificant book because it deals with the feelings of women talking together in a drawing room."

As Jude Kelly, the acclaimed British theater director, said in a TED talk,

Let me talk about *Hamlet*. "To be or not to be. That is the question." But it's not my question. My question is: Why was I taught as a young woman that this was the quintessential example of human dilemma and human experience? It is a great story, but it is a story about male conflict, male dilemma, male struggle. . . . We have to be prepared to go back through all our books and our films, all our favorite things, and say, actually, this is written by a male artist—not an artist. We have to see that so many of these stories are written through a male perspective. Which is fine, but then females need to have 50 percent of the rights for the stage, the film, the novel, the place of creativity.

A good way to measure the ubiquity of the male perspective masquerading as the human perspective is to check out the Nobel Prizes. The Nobel Prizes are awarded in six categories: literature, medicine, chemistry, peace, physics, and economics. Who we are as a species, what we value, where we expend our energy and our resources, and our priorities, goals, and dreams can be charted through the development of these categories. As of 2018, Nobel Prizes in total have been awarded to 853 men and 51 women. One hundred ten Nobel Prizes in Literature have been awarded since 1901, and only fourteen of those were awarded to women. The Nobel Prize in Medicine has been awarded to 198 men and 12 women; the Nobel Prize in Chemistry to 175 men and 5 women; the Nobel Peace Prize to 89 men, 17 women, and 24 organizations; the Nobel Prize in Physics to 206 men and 3 women; and the Nobel Prize in Economics to 50 men and 1 woman.

The world would have been different—and better—if women had had an equal say in the development of literature, medicine, chemistry, physics, peace, and economics. Better, not because women are better, but because they are more than half of humanity, representing more than half of what it means to be human. If you can convince me otherwise, you should receive a Nobel Prize.

KNOW
HER NAME

Tell me to what you pay attention,
and I will tell you who you are.

—JOSÉ ORTEGA Y GASSETT

Recently, I spent the night at a friend's house in New York City, and I got up early the next morning so I could walk through Central Park to a meeting in Midtown. I entered the park at Fifth Avenue and Sixty-Seventh Street and immediately came upon a large bronze statue. I had passed by this statue many times before, but I'd never stopped to examine it. It was a fine fall day, and I wasn't in a hurry, so this time I stopped and came close and read the inscription on the base of the monument: "Seventh Regiment New York, One Hundred and Seventh United States Infantry, in memoriam, 1917–1918." World War I. A war memorial. Seven larger-than-life soldiers, young men with their helmets, holding bayonets, one soldier carrying a dying, bloodied brother in his arms.

As I stood in front of the statue, I took in the whole scene: the autumn trees, the women and men rushing to work, the nannies pushing strollers, the traffic whirring and honking in the street. I thought how interesting, how strange, that humanity singles out war as the one form of boldness to memorialize. I kept walking, and before long I got to the Grand Army Plaza, the gateway to the park at Fifty-Ninth Street. There, rising tall above the crowd of pedestrians, was a statue of the Civil War Union general William Sherman, perched high on a horse, being led by an angel. Sherman is a somewhat polarizing historic figure. He is known for liberating the South from the Confederate Army, and he is also credited with the mass destruction of Atlanta during his notorious March to the Sea, as well as other scorched-earth tactics in the Civil War. He used that same military philosophy as commanding general of the Indian Wars. His policies included the first establishment of reservations, the killing of those who resisted relocation, and the starvation of remaining free-roaming Plains Indians by the mass eradication of buffalo herds.

Again, I stopped to behold this statue; it's hard *not* to pay attention to it. General Sherman, and his horse, and the angel, are covered completely in twenty-four-carat gold leaf. It's a gorgeous piece of art, created by the famous American sculptor Augustus Saint-Gaudens. I sat on a bench, studied the statue, and wondered, Why, of all the people in the world, does General Sherman get to sit on a gilded horse forever in Central Park? And why is this the same all around the world?

It doesn't matter where you are—in Paris passing the Arc de Triumph; in Volgograd, Russia, beholding the massive war statue *The Motherland Calls*; in Cambodia, in the temple ruins, where mile-long walls depict religious battles; or on the

Mall in our nation's capital. Wherever you are on this planet, it seems to have been decided long ago that history would be annotated by the warriors, and that courage, boldness, and strength would be associated with a willingness to fight and die—to put your life on the line for your ethnicity or religion or country.

I used to wonder about this as a kid. Why in school did we have to memorize the dates of a long list of battles and wars, or the names of the men who invented the atom bomb, but not the names of the people who invented things like washing machines, or solar panels, or birth control pills? Certainly, these discoveries (which, by the way, all involved women inventors and investors) also changed the course of history. Who chose violent conflict as the one human activity to laud over all others? Later on, when I was in college, getting my degree in education and doing my practice teaching in an inner-city school, I wondered, What if, alongside the marble tombs for the unknown soldiers, there were also monuments to the countless unheralded teachers who educate our children, keep them safe, prepare them as best they can to be good citizens?

When I became a midwife and I witnessed the courage of laboring women, I wondered, What if, next to a statue of a warrior holding his bloody comrade, sculptors had also been commissioned across the ages to represent a woman delivering a baby—strong and noble and, yes, bloody. Does that sound preposterous, gory, gross? Why? Blood is blood, whether it is spilled on the battlefield, as a young person dies, or in the delivery room, as new life is born. Now, I'm a realist—I know that human behavior can become so twisted that if allowed to reach a boiling point some kind of force is required to stop it. But that does not mean we should celebrate violent force as the penultimate definition of being bold, of being heroic. What happens to human consciousness when we memorize the dates of battles, and we pass the war memorials, and sing anthems with lyrics laced with bombs bursting in air?

José Ortega y Gassett, the nineteenth-century Spanish philosopher, said, "Tell me to what you pay attention, and I will tell you who you are." We have paid a lot of attention to violence and warriors. Search online for "the top ten events in American history." I did this. On the first site, all ten events were wars or attacks or assassinations. Same with the second list. The third list had the Apollo flight to the moon, plus nine violent incidents. Really? These are the events we want to know ourselves by? *Tell me to what you pay attention, and I will tell you who you are.* Tell me what would happen to us as a culture if a statue of Rosa Parks were placed right next to the Lincoln Memorial—and Miss Parks was as big and bold as the commander in chief? Or if next to the Vietnam War memorial there was a similar wall with thousands of names of the people who have honed other ways of dealing with conflict—like maybe communicating, forgiving, mediating? Working for justice so that the economic and social conditions that spawn unrest are transformed before they explode? How about monuments to the pioneers in mental health who are helping people heal internal wounds before they inflict external wounds on others? *Tell me to what you pay attention and I will tell you who you are.* Are we not also people who create shelters for those battered at home so their kids don't re-create the cycle of violence? Are we not also the caretakers of our culture—the nannies and home health aides and hospice workers; the farmers and earth stewards; the everyday citizens who feed and house and give jobs and hope to others?

There are twenty-nine sculptures in Central Park and not one honors historical women. A few feature female angels or dancing girls, and there's one of Alice in Wonderland and one of Mother Goose. Not that I have anything against angels, dancing girls, and fictional characters. But I was happy to learn that an organization called Monumental Women launched a campaign in 2014 to construct Central Park's first monument representing real women. Because of their persistence, the New York City Public Design Commission finally approved a statue honoring Susan B. Anthony, Elizabeth Cady Stanton, and Sojourner Truth. The monument will be the first in Central Park's 166-year history to depict real-life women and will celebrate the largest nonviolent revolution in our nation's history—the movement for women's right to vote. Won't it be great for little girls and boys to walk through the park and see those images and ask their parents, "Who are those ladies? What did they do? How did they do it?" *Tell me to what you pay attention, and I will tell you who you are.*

In December 2012, just weeks after the massacre at the Sandy Hook Elementary School in Newtown, Connecticut, I was invited to speak at a forum for townspeople who were drowning in shock and grief. A parent whose children attended the school had read my book *Broken Open*. She thought the message in the book might be a balm for the people of Newtown—the message that if we stay open during difficult times, as opposed to becoming hardened and bitter, we might stay afloat, we might find healing, and eventually we might find our way to a new shore, a new life. We might even use the pain for inner growth and for the betterment of our hurting world. I told the parent who invited me that it was probably still too early for those suffering such severe trauma and loss to consider anything but how to sleep at night, how to take one painful step after the other, how to breathe. Still, she wanted me to come, and so I accepted the invitation.

Since then, I have stayed in touch with many of those New-town parents and friends. I have watched with great admiration as they have chosen, over and over, to keep their hearts open, and not only to find their way to a new normal, but also to use the pain to fuel something good. To honor their children even as they mourn them every day. Recently, I went back to Newtown to speak again, at the invitation of two of the parents who founded a research and activism organization in their daughter's name—the Avielle Foundation.

Avielle was only six when the gunman took her life. I am calling him the "gunman" because I do not want to memorialize his name by mentioning it here. *Tell me to what you pay attention, and I will tell you who you are*. I never wanted to know his name. He left a trail of trauma and sorrow in his wake. His violence continues to ripple out. Just weeks after my last visit to Newtown I learned that Avielle's father had taken his own life, once again proving how violence begets more violence, and the cycle continues.

How do we break that cycle? One way is to change what we pay attention to—what deeds we honor and what names we know. There are many worthy names of people who meet adversity with love and optimism that never make it to the news. Instead, we are bombarded with the names of those who do harm. I am a news junkie. I read and watch and listen to the steady stream of negative stories every day. I feel it is my responsibility to stay informed. Throughout the ages, uninformed, head-in-the-clouds citizens have allowed motivated despots and hate mongers to rain travesties down on their communities and nations. An informed populace is the bedrock of democracy. But . . .

If all we do is immerse ourselves in the stories of bad people doing bad things to each other and the planet, we will sink under the weight of a lopsided story. We will feel alone and outnumbered, when really, there are so many people doing wildly imaginative, kind, and brave things at this very moment. This is why I try to eat a balanced news meal every day. You may have to search for the hopeful stories, but they are hiding in plain sight. Once you find them, you'll be so nourished you will want more, and you will want to share those stories, and even get involved. You will have less time for the nasty stories, the mean-spirited ones, the destructive ones. You'll want a creativity diet, a hope diet, a wisdom diet. You will not want to fill your mind with violent television shows and movies that are really glorified shoot-'em-up video games. You will get tired of superheroes that continue to meet violence with more violence. You will want to know the names of a different kind of superhero.

You will want to know her name: Antoinette Tuff. Do you know it? You should. She was the bookkeeper at an Atlanta elementary school who prevented another massive school shooting from happening. How did she do this? Not by being armed, not by threatening more violence. Rather, by staying in a small room and calmly communicating with a deranged twenty-year-old gunman, even though she had many opportunities to escape. For more than an hour she spoke to him from her heart, persuading him from using his loaded AK-47-style rifle on the hundreds of children right outside the room. "Don't feel bad, baby," she said, according to the tape of her 911 call. "We all suffer. My husband just left me after thirty-three years," she told the troubled young man. "I got a son with multiple disabilities. If I can get over tough times, so can you."

Later, when asked how she had done what she did, Ms. Tuff said she practiced what her pastor called anchoring. First anchoring in one's inner strength, and then letting empathy and compassion lead the way. "I just let him know he wasn't alone," she said. "I kept saying, baby, we don't want you to die today. You belong to us. Just put your guns down. I won't let anyone hurt you." And that's exactly what happened. He put the guns down, and Antoinette guided the SWAT team to come in gently and take him away. Anchored strength in service of compassion averted a national tragedy. But whereas stories that end in violence remain in the news for years, the very kind of action that worked—and could be funded and taught—was presented in the media as a sweet story and then lost after a few days. Antoinette Tuff. Anchored in strength and compassion. Know her name.

Malala Yousafzai. You may know her name already, but it's a name to keep on the tip of your tongue. She's the girl who was shot in the head by the Taliban because of her persistence in going to school and encouraging other girls in Pakistan. At a speech at the UN, on her sixteenth birthday, Malala spoke of love and education as the only remedies for hate and violence. She ended her remarkable speech by saying: "The Taliban shot me through my forehead. They shot my friends, too. They thought the bullets would silence us, but they failed. Out of the silence came thousands of voices. The terrorists thought they would change my aims and stop my ambitions. But nothing changed in my life except this: weakness, fear, and hopelessness died. Strength, power, and courage were born." Malala. Anchored in strength and compassion. Aware of a different kind of power. Know her name. Every time someone trots out a news story featuring the well-known name of a killer, or a criminal, or an elected official doing daily harm, say Malala's name. Tell her story.

Tammy Duckworth. There are so many reasons to know her name and to tell her story. She is a Purple Heart veteran who lost both of her legs in the Iraq War when her helicopter was struck by a rocket-propelled grenade in the autumn of 2004. She was the first disabled woman ever to be elected to the US House of Representatives, the second female Asian American to be elected to the Senate, and the first female senator to give birth while holding office. Of that first, she said, "It's about damn time. I can't believe it took until 2018. It says something about the inequality of representation that exists in our country." From her hospital bed after giving birth, she began to advocate for expanded parental-leave benefits, writing that "parenthood isn't just a women's issue, it's an economic issue and one that affects all parents—men and women alike. As tough as juggling the demands of motherhood and being a Senator can be, I'm hardly alone or unique as a working parent, and my children only make me more committed to doing my job and standing up for hardworking families everywhere."

Ten days later she rolled her wheelchair into the US Senate chamber to cast a vote, newborn baby in her lap. The Senate had, only the night before, voted unanimously to change the admission standards and allow Senator Duckworth to bring her child to work. That's my favorite reason to know Tammy Duckworth's name: she was the first woman or man to vote on the chamber floor holding her baby. Fearless in confronting archaic rules that diminish women's power, Duckworth was instrumental in changing the admission standards, allowing her and all mothers and fathers who also happen to be senators to bring their babies with them so as not to miss important votes. Similarly, she introduced the Friendly Airports for Mothers Act that compels large airports to include lactation areas for traveling mothers. She is committed to changing the story about motherhood, fatherhood, and work.

When I saw the image of Senator Duckworth wheeling herself onto the Senate floor, I was brought to tears. That image told a new story. A disabled, Asian American, nursing mother, who was just doing her job, and doing it passionately, excellently, vocally, and proudly.

Tell me to what you pay attention, and I will tell you who you are.

I search the news, and I search my town and workplace, for names to pay attention to so that we might change the story of who we are. I want to know the names of people anchored in strength and compassion. "I've never been interested in evil," Toni Morrison said, "but stunned by the attention given to its every whisper." It's up to us to deny evil the attention it seeks. It's up to us to demand stories of love and justice, to read and watch them, to validate and elevate them. To pay attention to the women and men who are doing power differently, and to know their names.

LEAVING
THE CAVE

It wasn't just a bunch of guys out there

chasing bison around.

—DEAN SNOW

Some years ago, my husband and I traveled to the Périgord region of France, and to its beautiful river valleys and cliffs where our Cro-Magnon ancestors drew their stories on the walls of limestone caves. I had always wanted to visit those caves and to view the prehistoric art that is said to be between ten thousand and thirty-five thousand years old. I had seen the images in magazines and books—the paintings of panthers, bison, wooly mammoths, rhinoceros, and horses. The shapes of women's bodies carved into the stone. The mysterious symbols scratched on the walls. The handprints. The hands of the artists, our first storytellers.

There are all sorts of theories about the art—that the animal paintings were made by hunters as supplications for a bountiful hunt, or maybe they were the work of the first warriors, telling the stories of survival in a dangerous wilderness.

Some archaeologists believe the art was made by shamans who went deep into the caves to conduct rituals and connect with the spirit world. They left on the walls the earliest renderings of our ancestors' search for meaning—the remnants of a religion, some surmise, that centered around fertility, motherhood, and nature. There was one thing the scholars and field archaeologists agreed on—that the prehistoric artists were men.

One day, sitting in the waiting room at the dentist's office, I was flipping through a *National Geographic* magazine and I came across an article with this headline: "Women Created Most of the Oldest-Known Cave Art Paintings, Suggests a New Analysis of Ancient Handprints. Most Scholars Had Assumed These Ancient Artists Were Predominantly Men, So the Finding Overturns Decades of Archaeological Dogma." The article was about the work of Dean Snow, a Penn State archaeologist whose research was supported by the National Geographic Society's Committee for Research and Exploration.

According to the article, Snow "analyzed hand stencils found in eight cave sites in France and Spain. By comparing the relative lengths of certain fingers, Snow determined that three-quarters of the handprints were female. 'There has been a male bias in the literature for a long time,' said Snow. . . . 'People have made a lot of unwarranted assumptions about who made these things, and why.'" But Snow suggested that women were involved in every aspect of prehistoric life—from the hunt to the hearth to religious ritual. "It wasn't just a bunch of guys out there chasing bison around," he said.

That was it! Now I had to go to France to see the caves. And so, my husband and I did just that. We settled into a little hotel, perched on a hill above an ancient town, where the calm waters of the Vézère and Dordogne rivers meet. We spent a week exploring the caves (and eating French food and drinking red wine). We visited caves large and small—some public, some located on a farmer's field. You step into the cool interior of a cave, and for a moment everything is completely dark. Then the park guide or the farmer shines a light and suddenly you have traveled back as much as thirty-five thousand years to a time when panthers and rhinoceros roamed the land. There on the walls are those mysterious symbols, the handprints, the round breasts and bellies of pregnant women, and the artistically rendered images of animals.

At night, after drinking a quality (and quantity) of wine we never did back home, I would read aloud to my husband about the Cro-Magnon population who painted on the walls of the caves we had visited earlier in the day. It seemed that everything we had learned about "cavemen" in school or from watching *The Flintstones* was incomplete and misleading. Who were these people who retreated deep into the womb-like caves to paint stories about their interwoven relationship with nature and animals, birth and death? The image I had formed of crude, hairy men holding clubs and grunting around a fire did not match up with the images on the cave walls. And what about cavewomen? No one ever seemed to mention them. Why had we been led to believe that our ancestors were merely violent survivalists bent on protection and conquest? What about the mothers and caretakers, the artists and the mystics and the healers whose hands had painted and molded the cave art? Their handprints were on the walls of the caves, but Cro-Magnon cavewomen had not made it into our history books.

In one regional guidebook, I read this:

> The Cro-Magnon paid homage to a number of
> goddesses who were associated with the fertility of
> the earth, as well as the moon and the stars. One great
> goddess linked to the moon was carved in limestone
> over the entrance to an underground cathedral in
> Laussel, France, perhaps 20,000 years ago. She was
> painted in the colors of life and fertility: blood red. Her
> left hand still rests upon her pregnant belly whereas
> in her right hand she holds the horned crescent of
> the moon, which is engraved with thirteen lines, the
> number of new moon cycles in a solar year. She was a
> goddess of life, linked to the mysteries of the heavens
> and the magical powers of the moon whose 29-day
> cycle likely corresponded with the Cro-Magnon
> menstrual cycle which issues from a woman's life-
> giving womb.

Not only had the first storytellers been women, but many of their stories were about women—their bodies, their values, the validity of what they did and knew and cared about. Why had the fullness of our ancestors' consciousness stayed behind in the caves? Like so many stories from history, and especially the ones about early humans and indigenous peoples, the focus has been on our inherited violent, warlike nature, as if we need that story to brace the scaffolding around our agreement of just-the-way-it-is. But what about the stories of the earliest human urge to care for each other, to parent, to cook and nurse, to love and create? Why were those so-called soft storylines overlooked and not told alongside the warrior stories? Why were they not held up as critical aspects of the human journey through time? Why have those stories stayed in the caves—and not just those prehistoric caves but in the forgotten rooms of every era?

I wondered this each day of our trip, as we drove through the countryside, where the artifacts of the ongoing human story are layered in the towns on the riverbanks. In the architecture you see the shifting influence of different peoples—Celts, Romans, Moors, French, English. You see evidence of periods of relative peace and prosperity, and times of war, famine, and revolts. In one little town we stood in the garden of a simple stone church that featured a statue of the Virgin Mary. We looked across the river to a towering castle perched on a cliff, fortified to protect against invasion. A sign in the church garden paid homage to people who had died during the Black Plague, when 60 percent of Europe's population was wiped out. What were the lives of the people really like during each of these epochs? What were the relationships like, the marriages, the dynamics between women and men, between friends and families? What did the people eat and create, and wonder and fear? What went on in the hearts of real people? Everything I knew about European history had to do with wars and kings, trade routes and power plays between religions, royalty, and tyrants. Why did we only know and care about these aspects of being human?

Standing in that medieval garden, I had an experience like those deathbed visions when they say your whole life passes in front of your eyes and you finally connect all the dots. In this case I saw the march of history pass before us. I saw what had made it into the history books and what had been left out. I understood how what we modern Westerners believe is just the way it is, is merely a sliver of time, a slice of the whole story. Being in the caves, seeing the handprints of the first storytellers and their images of fertile women and dancing animals, I got a visceral experience of how history is often a distorted window into the past, the perspective of those with the power to tell it. And once again I was reminded of the opportunity we have to participate in changing the narrative.

On the last day of the trip we came upon a little farm on a back road. A handwritten sign in the yard said *Peintures Rupestres*—cave paintings. We knocked on the door of the farmhouse, and a stooped old man answered. He showed us a battered photograph of cave art and named a price to see it. After we paid up, he got his coat and a flashlight and motioned for us to follow. Taking our hands, he pulled us both across the rutted field behind his barn. He smelled of dirt and sweat and alcohol, and he mumbled to me about je ne sais quoi since I barely understand French.

We arrived at the mouth of a small cave. The farmer explained something, pushing my husband and me into the opening. Inside, it was pitch-dark, dank, and moist. Suddenly, the farmer groped around for my arm, pulled me toward him, put his hands on my breasts, and rubbed his body against mine. I froze. I tried to say something, but I had lost my voice. Before

I had a chance to find it again, the farmer pushed me away and turned on the flashlight. He sidled up to my husband and proceeded to point out two roughly scratched images of horses that looked as if they had been carved into the soft sandstone by his children.

Repelled and claustrophobic, I grabbed my husband's hand and we stumbled toward the opening of the cave. Once outside, as we walked back across the field to the car, I told him what had happened. He wanted to go back and give the guy a talking-to, but I just wanted to leave. I've thought about that moment in the farmer's cave many times, and how it could have become the only story I told about our trip to the Périgord. But I don't want that one piece of a bigger tale to be what I remember. I don't want the worst of mankind to stand out above the beauty and the goodness. I want to remember the delicious food and wine that the couple who ran our hotel fed us every night when we returned from our adventures. I want to remember the way the region is painstakingly protecting the art in the caves. I want to remember and tell the story of the flower markets, the chestnuts being harvested, the trees being tended, the children in the school yard, the lovers in the town square, the vineyards, the sunflowers, the lace curtains in our room.

That trip shifted something in me. I began to let myself imagine how things would be different now if the whole story had made it out of the caves—if the voices and values of the first storytellers had prevailed, or at least been included. What if our myths and teaching tales had purposely led humanity to believe that it was the ultimate sign of strength to nurture and love? What if the urge to care for children and nature and each other had been chosen as the most important tasks of any society? What if care as opposed to conquest had been the marker of virility? What if resources were granted to the people most skilled at peacemaking, healing, creating, and opposed to those with brute strength and a penchant for violence?

At the end of the article about the research of Dean Snow, the archaeologist who analyzed the handprints of the Cro-Magnon artists, Snow says that his work raises questions that archaeologists will be debating for years to come. But the question Snow says he gets most often is why these ancient artists left handprints at all. "I have no idea," he says, "but a pretty good hypothesis is that this is somebody saying, 'This is mine, I did this.'" When I think about the human story that needs updating more than any other, it is the story of power, the story I examine in Part II of this book. It is time for women to change that story, to leave our handprints, to say, "This is mine, I did this."

PART II

POWER STORIES

If women are not perceived
to be fully within the structures of power,
surely it is power that we need to redefine
rather than women.

—*Mary Beard*

Power. It's been so abused that it feels like a dirty word. But what is it actually? Power is a natural force, and it's something we all want: the energy, the freedom, the authority to be who we are, to contribute, to create. Domination and control have become synonymous with power, but power does not have to come at the expense of others; it does not have to oppress in order to express. The urges to subjugate, punish, or annihilate are corrupted versions of power.

All of us want to shine as brightly as we can. It's as if we come into this world bearing a spark, one that longs to be fanned into a flame of authentic selfhood. There is nothing inherently domineering about that pure desire to shine, nothing in it that must suck up all the oxygen and extinguish the other flames. There is a way to reveal one's shining self without diminishing the light of another. There is a way to do power differently than the way we have come to define it.

I've been exploring, researching, and living out questions about power—and especially about women and power—my whole life. This probably started because of the predominantly female household of my childhood—mother, grandmother, great-aunt, sisters—and my father, the one man, the sun in the family system whose authority eclipsed everyone else's. I am the second daughter of four girls, and for reasons I have never figured out, I was the dissenter. Even as a child I was aware of the exclusive power granted my father by our house full of girls and women. It disturbed me that my mother—my smart, ambitious, beautiful mother—bought into my father's delusions of superiority. At least I thought they were delusions. It was quite obvious to me that the system was rigged in favor of just one of us, for the sole reason of his gender. I never understood why my mother tolerated my father's humiliations. Or why she was expected to participate in his interests, projects, and adventures, while he made fun of hers. And ours. It was a given that whatever he wanted to do, we would do, no questions asked, no complaints tolerated. Any plans "the girls" could cook up—from school events to social activities—were silly and inconsequential in the eyes of my father. I couldn't wait to get away from the unfairness of it all.

As it turned out, I met up with the same gendered dynamics wherever I went—in college, in social circles, and especially at work. Although I had cofounded my organization, it seemed that gender inequity was just the air we all breathed, and I felt the same resentment I had felt as a girl. My priorities were undervalued, and more often than not my ability to influence important decisions and budgets were obstructed. I attributed some of this to the fact that I was a woman and therefore not taken seriously by my male colleagues. But as the years went on it began to dawn on me that in order to change the story of power in my world, I was going to have to make some changes in myself. I was going to have to dredge up my personal power—my inner strength, my inherent dignity, my self-worth. Easier said than done. Layers and layers of self-doubt, unexplored and unexpressed anger, and a slew of other problems were covering my authentic power.

First, there was the problem of likability. I had bought into the notion that, as a woman, it was part of my job description to be nice, agreeable, likable *all the time*. I feared that if I voiced my opinions too often or lobbied hard for what I thought was right—for the organization, for other staff members, and God forbid, for myself—people may not like me. I could hear ancient warnings being whispered in my ear: *Look what happened to Eve! Remember Cassandra. Don't be like them. Stay small, be quiet, be nice.*

Then there was the problem of the "imposter syndrome." Who was I to make demands? What did I know about running a business? Omega Institute had grown into a complex organization. More than twenty-five thousand people attended our programs each year. We hosted hundreds of workshops, conferences, trainings, and retreats led by some of the leading thinkers in the world. I was young and inexperienced and learning on the job. Of course, the men I was working with were nursing insecurities of their own, and they were certainly as inexperienced and mistake-prone as I was, but somehow, they felt entitled to speak up for what they believed in. They followed their instincts; they made their points; they got what they wanted. When I would try to do the same thing, I was accused of whining or complaining or being manipulative. My priorities were demeaned as idealistic, soft, and just not as important as I thought they were.

Most of the time I wasn't even part of the conversation because I got tired of playing a game that didn't come naturally to me. I didn't relate to the rules of engagement. I wanted to converse so as to understand differing points of view. I wasn't looking to prevail. That was not the game I wanted to play. I thought that if each of us brought our strengths to the table, admitted our weaknesses, and filled in the gaps for one another, we all could learn and grow and help the business thrive. If we all conceded and compromised when it was called for, we could share the power. But I seemed to be the one who did most of the conceding and compromising—my priorities, my salary, my title, my role. I pushed my anger underground, but it made its way up to the surface anyway in ineffective outbursts and backdoor manipulations.

I didn't have the words for it then, but now I know what was going on: I was a woman trying to excel and contribute within a system built by and for men. I was like women the world over in all sorts of work environments. We were spending so much of our energy and intelligence trying to get a foot in the old door that by the time we got into the room, *we* had changed, but the structures had stayed the same "If women are not perceived to be fully within the structures of power," writes the historian Mary Beard, "surely it is power that we need to redefine rather than women."

But how to change a structure while living under its roof? I didn't know how and I didn't know where to look for inspiration or help. I was beyond tired of those how-to business books that encouraged women to lean in, to leave behind their instincts and needs, and to squash their authenticity into an ill-fitting persona. And it wasn't just in business. Politics, religion, activism, academia, sports, entertainment: women were indeed entering more fields, but the cost to their personhood, their values, their families, was high. Of course, the cost to a woman's personhood and family had been high for working-women long before this current influx into the job market. But with more and more women in the workforce, more and more glaring inequities were coming to the fore.

For example, why if women were sharing the workload *outside* of the home weren't men expected to share the work *within* the home? And why were women still being paid less than men for doing the same jobs? Why were the jobs that many men held valued more than the jobs many women did? Plumbers paid more than home-health-care providers, correctional officers paid more than teachers. And who cared if women actors were getting roles in blockbuster films if the scripts featured the same old car chases and gun battles? All of this seemed to me less like a triumph of women's empowerment and more like a victory for an imbalanced value system and an incomplete vision of life. Was this really the best we could do?

I knew we could do better. I knew I could do better, but I didn't know how, especially since I felt isolated in my frustration. That was why, in 2002, I convened a women's conference at Omega. The idea for the conference came to me while I was doing something else, which was the story of my life back then, and the story of women's lives forever—the original multitaskers doing both the paid and the unpaid labor. By then I was divorced, remarried, and the mother of three teenagers. Late one night I was home folding a mountain of clean clothes, an activity I have always found comforting. Anyone who has done laundry for a family knows what lurks at the bottom of the pile:

a slew of incompatible socks. Where have their mates gone? It's like a Zen koan: Where in the world is the other sock? A koan has no real answer, and neither did the sock mystery, so I would just make random pairings and roll the misfits into little balls, assuming my kids would never notice the difference.

This night, as I matched the unmatchable, I was thinking of a recurring struggle I was having at work, a struggle so many women were experiencing then, and still are: I was a creative force at my organization, and yet I wasn't being paid or acknowledged proportionately. The lack of financial parity was deeply unfair and majorly consequential, but what bothered me even more was my own discomfort—even my shame—around the issue of power. The old messages about women and power rang in my head like an ancient gong, still vibrating from the past. Messages that made me question my worth. Admonishments to stay silent or to preface what I said with a justification. Old story lines that told me that it was the woman's role to keep the peace, to smooth egos, to do the emotional labor, yet at the same time those endeavors were unseen and unpaid. I only vaguely sensed what was going on. Therefore, I said yes when I meant no. I took on work that wasn't mine to do. I didn't say what I knew because I didn't trust what I knew: that my way of doing things, my instincts, my priorities were valid; that I myself was valuable and should be paid accordingly. My attempts at explaining all of this were anemic and often had the effect of disempowering me even more. But if the only way to claim power was to become like those who were denying me what I deserved, I didn't want it anyway.

Women and power . . . what a conundrum. This is what I

was thinking about sitting in the quiet house, bunching together the socks. Somewhere in the back of my mind I sensed the presence of millions of other women who were experiencing similar issues and were equally unsettled by those two words. *Women* and *power*. The words were like the socks: mismatched. They were a koan looking for an answer.

As I carried the laundry basket upstairs, I said the words. It made me anxious hearing my voice barely whisper them. It was just my husband and boys asleep in the house, but still, I was afraid someone would hear me and think I was a woman who wanted power. Then it occurred to me—now, that would make a great conference. Putting those words together and asking ourselves why the pairing was so troubling. Saying things out loud that women had been wondering for ages: What is power anyway? Who gets to have it, use it, define it? Can it be shared? Does it always corrupt? Can a person wield power without violence and domination? Can women usher in an era of doing power differently? Can we all talk about this?

I began to discuss the subject with the authors and speakers who came to Omega each season. I had conversations with mythologists, psychologists, feminists, biologists, brain researchers, nuns, artists, and business leaders. I paid closer attention to the discomfort as well as the growing courage within me, my friends, my colleagues, and women in the news as we all reckoned with female power and its expression. Finally, I wove all those strings together into Omega's first conference on the subject, called, simply, Women & Power.

My colleagues and I (important note: two of them were open-minded, supportive men) invited a few speakers whose work epitomized the courage it was going to take for women not merely to claim power but also to redefine it. They included Anita Hill, whose testimony before Congress hearkened back to Cassandra's story, and Eve Ensler, creator of the ground-breaking play *The Vagina Monologues*. I figured maybe fifty people would attend the conference. Several hundred showed up. The next year we offered it again, this time pairing founding mothers of the women's movement with younger speakers. We sold out. The next year we held the conference in New York City, and two thousand women came from around the world.

Since then I have organized many gatherings and spoken at others, exploring the themes of women and power, women and peace, women and work, women and men. I have listened to stories, gathered information and statistics, and learned about doing power differently from leaders, artists, activists, and everything in between—from a NASA astronaut to a revolutionary nun, to women on both sides of the abortion debate, and to women and men in conversation about changing the story together. Their stories, their experiences, their struggles and victories have inspired many, myself included, to dig deep to reclaim our authentic brand of power so that we can make real change in our own spheres of influence.

Women have an advantage as power outsiders for most of recorded history to step in now and question some basic assumptions: that domination and violence are necessary to maintain order; that men are divinely or biologically predetermined to lead; and that the strong and silent warrior is to be revered while the emotional, communicative caretaker is second-rate. Do we really want to break the glass ceilings just to end up in that old story? If that's all we do, we'll just get more of what no longer works. Or, as we gain influence at home, at work, and in the world, do we want to shake the foundation of the whole story? As women claim power—as we become protagonists in the stories that shape our world—we must keep asking these questions: Power for what purpose? Influence, why? Promotion, money, leadership, to what end?

What are we going to use our power for?

THE OLD STORY OF POWER

*The great force of history comes from the fact
that we carry it within us,
are unconsciously controlled by it. . . .
History is literally present in all that we do.*

—JAMES BALDWIN

Whenever I write anything—an article, a speech, a book—I do what many people do before jumping into a creative project. I freeze up. I doubt myself. I employ common strategies of avoidance: I "research" online, when in reality I make music mixes on Spotify or shop for kitchen gadgets. I cook. I eat. One of my favorite ways to procrastinate while not writing is to clean—my car, the refrigerator, closets.

One summer, a month or so before that year's Women & Power conference, I tried to turn my attention to writing a speech about redefining power. I was met with a sudden urge to clean the basement of our house. It had been calling to me for years, but it's dank and kind of scary down there, so I had let things pile up—old toys and memorabilia, ancient computers, winter boots and broken chairs, cardboard boxes growing moldy with age.

Now was a perfect time to tackle the mess since my husband—the pack rat—was out of town, unable to impede my penchant for throwing stuff away. I had high hopes of filling a dumpster while avoiding writing. My idea of a good time. I went down the stairs and surveyed piles of junk and stacks of boxes. First step: open each box, determine the contents, and separate the disposable from the salvageable.

I pulled the packing tape off the first box. It was full of books belonging to my youngest son. He had recently graduated from St. John's College, which is also called the Great Books School. Over the course of four years every student reads the same hundred books—the canon of Western thought—often referred to by the students as "the dead white man's curriculum."

I picked up the first book in the box. It was *The Prince*, by Niccolò Machiavelli, written in 1532.

"Don't open it," I said to myself. "Don't go down that rabbit hole."

I knew all cleaning would come to a halt if I started reading anything in the basement—an old *National Geographic* magazine, the manual to our washing machine, or *The Prince*. But I couldn't help myself. I had never read *The Prince*. I was aware that Machiavelli championed the kind of leadership that shunned morality and empathy. I knew his quote about the ends justifying the means. But why was his book part of the St. John's curriculum? Why was it one of the one hundred greatest books of the Western canon? I opened *The Prince* to a random page. My eyes fell on this line: "When considering power, it is better to be feared than loved, if you cannot be both." Wow. That's pretty heavy, I thought. That's exactly why we need to do power differently. Maybe I should read this. I flipped through the pages until I came to another disturbing bit of advice: "It is better to be adventurous than cautious, because fortune is a woman, and if you want to keep her under, it is necessary to beat and ill-use her." I bookmarked that page and slammed *The Prince* shut.

The next book in the box was Aristotle's *The Politics*. I opened it and scanned the first pages. That classic book also contained shockingly misogynistic stuff about power and leadership. I put that on top of *The Prince* for further study. Then I rummaged through the box: *Selected Essays* by Karl Marx; *The Wealth of Nations* by Adam Smith; and a whole slew of other books by dead white men: Plato and Plutarch, Augustine and Saint Paul, Thomas Hobbes, John Locke, and the fathers of American democracy. I opened each book and read paragraphs and whole pages. It was as if I had come across the "23 and Me" DNA record of patriarchal power. Talk about Pandora's box, I said to myself. *This* was the dangerous box!

I pulled out another book. It was a big one, with a bold red cover. *The 48 Laws of Power*, by Robert Greene. I recognized the book; it had been on bestseller lists a few years back. I opened to the preface and read the first lines:

The feeling of having no power over people and events is generally unbearable to us—when we feel helpless we feel miserable. No one wants less power; everyone wants more. In the world today, however, it is dangerous to seem too power hungry, to be overt with your power moves. We have to seem fair and decent. So we need to be subtle—congenial yet cunning, democratic yet devious.

At first, I thought the author was kidding. Maybe this was a spoof, the kind of book that kids at St. John's read for comic relief. But as I read on, I realized the author was dead serious.

There was an old rocking chair—the chair I had nursed my babies in—in the corner of the basement. It was missing one of its rockers, but I pulled it across the room anyway, to a spot under a bare lightbulb. As I sat in that off-kilter chair, it wasn't lost on me how wacky the scene would have looked to someone else. A broken nursing chair, a moldy basement, a woman reading a book called *The 48 Laws of Power*.

Greene had compiled centuries of thought into one manual, quoting and synthesizing the works of the "masters of power," as he called them, from Machiavelli to Mao Tse-tung, from Sun Tzu to Socrates. His 48 Laws included these: Law #2—Never Put Too Much Trust in Friends, Learn How to Use Enemies; Law #4—Always Say Less Than Necessary; Law #7—Get Others to Do the Work for You, But Always Take the Credit; Law #17—Keep Others in Suspended Terror: Cultivate an Air of Unpredictability; Law #20—Do Not Commit to Anyone; Law #42—Strike the Shepherd and the Sheep Will Scatter.

I was dumbfounded. I suddenly felt so naive. You mean to say there was a method to the madness of the abuse of power? Why hadn't I gotten the memo?

Before I knew it, it was late afternoon. I had spent the day in the basement, talking to myself, folding the corners of pages, sampling that one box of books. I put them all back in the moldy box and carried it upstairs. I wiped off each book, starting with *The Prince*, cleared a shelf in my writing room, and arranged the books in chronological order. That was the end of my cleaning project and the beginning of a deep dive into the story of power. As I read through the books I had retrieved from the basement, I was reminded that a certain kind of person, a certain kind of man, has told the tales of power through the ages, and if we want to change that story, we have to know it—its origins and purpose, its winners and losers, its spoken and unspoken rules. And so, I set about reading its sacred texts—the "origin stories" and the "greatest books" of power.

I started with *The Art of War*, an ancient treatise dating from the fifth century BCE. Written by the Chinese military general Sun Tzu, *The Art of War* is probably the most universally mentioned text when it comes to defining and using power. Most recently, the business community has dusted the book off and incorporated its philosophy and strategies into leadership manuals and catchy memes. In the book, the words *war* and *leadership* are interchangeable, because, according to Sun Tzu, "to maintain order a leader must expect to wage war."

The two most often occurring key words from *The Art of War* are *fear* and *deception*. Those were the tactics Sun Tzu urged a leader to use because, he said, there were only two kinds of people in a leader's world—subjects and enemies. He wrote: "If they fear you, they will respect you. If they love you, they might respect you. But if they don't fear you, they'll never love you or respect you." And this one: "Pretend inferiority and encourage his arrogance. All warfare is based on deception."

Fear, deception, arrogance, attack, annihilation—these are the strategies of power according to Sun Tzu, and not only for military power but for every endeavor in every realm, from the home to the markets to the king's court.

For me, reading *The Art of War* was like being a fly on the wall in the locker room of power. I had multiple aha moments as I affixed the faces of specific leaders—past and present, political and personal—to the behaviors and strategies Sun Tzu promoted. The same thing happened when I read *The Prince*, the other book that is essential to the prevailing definition of power.

Niccolò Machiavelli wrote *The Prince* in 1532. Some say he introduced a new idea into Western culture—that morality has no place in the leadership arena. But actually, Machiavelli was just being an honest reporter of what had been going on for centuries. He wrote: "It must be understood that a leader cannot observe all of those virtues for which men are reputed good, because it is often necessary to act against mercy, against faith, against humanity, against frankness, in order to preserve order." He echoed Sun Tzu's philosophy with this directive: "Men are less hesitant about harming someone who makes himself loved than one who makes himself feared; fear is sustained by dread of punishment which will never abandon you."

Machiavelli believed that all men would be wise to develop the character of a prince. Whether at home as the head of a family, or running a business, or a nation, he boldly stated what others—especially church leaders of the times—pretended to abhor: that a leader will get ahead by being self-interested rather than caring about others; that it is more effective to be punishing as opposed to merciful. And that honesty had no real place in the halls of power. It is better, Machiavelli said, for a man to break promises if keeping them would thwart his success.

As I made my way through the basement box of books— from China, Japan, Greece, Rome, Europe, America—a few things stood out: the focus on domination and aggression; the linkage of leadership and war; and the nonexistence of women's voices and concerns. I found myself wondering, What would it be like for humanity today if women had contributed to the theories and stories about what it meant to be a powerful person? What if the skills women had developed over the centuries had been as revered as the skills of men? What if their emotional intelligence, their relational natures, their roles as nurturers, healers, mothers, and teachers had been respected, sought after, and woven into to the story of power?

Of course, there would be problems if women had been the only storytellers, the only ones to set examples and define reality. But if women's voices had been equally sought and valued, there would be other stories to balance out the ones about slaying dragons and waging war. A hero would not only be the one who went on crusades and adventures. If women had also been the protagonists of societies' teaching tales, swords in stones and bombs bursting in air would have been no more laudatory than educating children and tending the garden. Acts like rape and pillage, violence and brute force would have never been associated with the "hero's journey." The culture would not only revere the strong and silent type; it would also be cool to be talkative, brave to cry, noble to feel and relate.

Had that happened, the story of power would have been a more balanced one, a more inclusive one; it would not be a "single story," in the words of the author Chimamanda Ngozi Adichie. She writes, "The single story creates stereotype and the problem with stereotypes is not that they are untrue but that they are incomplete, they make one story become the only story." The single story of power has not only hurt and left women out of the equation. Anyone who doesn't live up to the stereotypes is marginalized. And any value that is outside the realm of the old story of power is considered weak.

The single story of power—the excess of one value system and the exclusion of others—has left humanity in a bind. It's not as simple as empowering those who have been left out of the story. We need new stories that arise from different values. We need new ways of dealing with stubborn problems long in the making: violence and war, environmental degradation, population strain, economic disparity, racism, sexism, hunger, poverty.

Albert Einstein is often quoted as saying, "No problem can be solved from the same consciousness that created it." He also is quoted as saying, "The definition of insanity is doing the same thing over and over again and expecting different results." While I heartily believe both of those quotes, Einstein said neither of them. The other day I searched for exactly what he did say about solving intractable problems, but before I found what I was looking for, I came across this: "Don't believe everything you read on the internet just because there is a picture of me with a quote by it. —Albert Einstein"

What Einstein did say is this: "A new type of thinking is essential if mankind is to survive and move to higher levels. Often in evolutionary processes a species must adapt to new conditions in order to survive. Today we must abandon competition and secure cooperation. This must be the central fact in all our considerations . . . otherwise we face certain disaster."

Given his track record solving a few tricky cosmological problems, I think it wise to take Professor Einstein's words to heart when he says that a new type of thinking is essential if mankind is to survive and move to higher levels. What might power look like if generated from a new type of thinking? New thinking would reject the parts of Sun Tzu's and Machiavelli's worldviews that glorify fear, deception, arrogance, attack, and annihilation. New-thinking leaders would be bold and decisive but would regard violence as the tactic of cowards, and war as a lack of imagination. They would seek to understand and guide, as opposed to dominate or punish. They would lean toward inclusion; they would not want others to fear them. I think Einstein would agree with me.

When I say we need new-thinking leaders, that's different from saying we need women to lead. All genders are capable of being wise and open and communicative, of shaping a new power story. But I believe a whole lot of women have ready access to this consciousness if we trust who we are and say what we know.

Women may have inclinations toward these qualities, but that is no guarantee that we will use them when the going gets tough, when the issues get complex, when crises and disagreements loom. Real and abiding consciousness change doesn't just happen. We have to work for it—in the world and within our own hearts and minds. No one, woman or man, is immune to the allure of the old power story. It's the only story that's been told about power, so within each of us is our own version of Sun Tzu, our own mini-Machiavelli. It takes work to recognize that part of the self and to tame it.

Just because women were not given the chance to add their voices to the storytelling doesn't mean we haven't colluded with the story line. And just because women have the potential to think differently doesn't mean we will. Yes, the research shows that women have honed more caring and collaborative instincts; we nurture relationships and connectivity; we are less likely to use violence to deal with conflict. But all people harbor within them a full range of human impulses and reactions, some noble and some ignoble. All of us have baser instincts—the urge to manipulate or dominate, to be selfish and unkind, to unfairly blame or shame, to walk over others so we can get what we need. Egocentricity is genderless.

It is critical that women are honest about this, that we are self-aware, and that as we try to change the world around us, we also pay attention to the world within us. If we think it's only an "outside job," or if we insist that only others must change—men, those with power and privilege, whole systems—we will repeat history and be corrupted by the very power we have the opportunity to transform.

"Stories can break the dignity of a people," writes Chimamanda Ngozi Adichie. "But stories can also repair that broken dignity." If we want to repair the dignity of those left out of the single story of power, and if we want to tell a more inclusive and innovative one, an important step is to look within, and do some repair work from the inside out—to redignify ourselves and to cultivate a consciousness that is different from the one that created the problems in the first place, to paraphrase Professor Einstein. It will require honest self-reflection, and the ability to self-correct when our old-story power urges—our mini-Machiavellis—are activated.

Besides the very real, very stubborn obstacles of sexism, racism, classism, protectionism, and a whole slew of other social and structural impediments to women's empowerment, there exist equally real and stubborn obstacles within us. Women have internalized patriarchy and created unhealthy coping mechanisms to survive and prosper within the existing laws of power. If we no longer want to collude with those laws, and if we want to be cocreators of a new story, some of the work starts on the inside with what C. G. Jung called shadow work, a process I explore next.

WOMEN, POWER, AND THE SHADOW

Whoever fights monsters,
should see to it that in the process
he does not become a monster.

—FRIEDRICH NIETZSCHE

All my life I've toggled between being an activist—someone interested in healing and changing the world around me—and an *innervist*, a word I made up to describe the part of me that seeks inner change, inner healing. I've never regarded activism and *innervism* as mutually exclusive. In fact, one keeps the other in check. If we focus only on fighting what we perceive to be wrong *out there*, we miss out on the very real work waiting to be done within our own hearts and minds and lives. If we don't look at our blind spots, our projections, our hypocrisies, we can end up doing what Friedrich Nietzsche warned against: "Whoever fights monsters," Nietzsche said, "should see to it that in the process he does not become a monster."

We see this every day: the very people spouting tolerance and inclusivity becoming intolerant and insular; or those pushing "family values" in public acting out the opposite in their private lives; or the revolutionaries, after the revolution, turning into the tyrants they toppled. And we see it in our own lives. I see it in mine. Like when I proclaim that women are capable of changing the human story—helping it become a more kind, just, and peaceful one, and then I fail to bring those very qualities into my daily relationships at work and home. This is where innervism comes in: taking responsibility for how I behave; recognizing my own flawed nature so that I can forgive others their imperfections, too; walking the talk; *being* the change.

When speaking of women and power, we need to talk about both innervism and activism. Innervism, because women hold personal and collective pain in their bodies and souls that needs healing from the inside out. Activism because there are indeed monsters in this world who need to be confronted now. There is evil. There is cruelty, greed, and injustice. I use the word *activism* to describe any call you answer to confront those monsters, anything you do to serve a cause greater than yourself. Your activism might look like joining a political campaign, a social-justice movement, the school board, the local fire department. Or being a foster parent, or a therapist, or someone who picks up litter on the side of a road. Activism is "love made visible," as Kahlil Gibran wrote. Love of people, animals, trees, community, country, land, planet.

Innervism is love of oneself. It is the realization that healing the self and healing the world go hand in hand. It is a way of remembering that sometimes the monsters dwell within. Sometimes the very evils we want to fight in the world, the broken behaviors we blame on others, are also alive in us and in need of our attention, our kindness, our understanding, our healing. Sometimes what we long to see changed in the world is an inside job.

By innervism you may think I am referring to a type of relaxing self-care. Certainly some inner work is like that. It is good and necessary to care gently and kindly for our bodies and hearts and nervous systems. I am talking about a different kind of innervism here. Becoming aware of the "monster within" has not been a day at the spa for me. It has been hard work. The Swiss psychologist C. G. Jung used the term *shadow work* to describe this kind of innervism.

There are many excellent books about shadow work. I recommend those by the Jungian psychologists Robert Johnson and Marion Woodman and by the poet Robert Bly. I especially like the way author Scott Jeffrey summarizes the work here, taken from his online guide, "A Definitive Guide to Jungian Shadow Work":

> It's always standing right behind us, just out of view.
> In any direct light, we cast a shadow. The shadow is
> a psychological term for everything we can't see in
> ourselves. Most of us go to great lengths to protect our
> self-image from anything unflattering or unfamiliar.
> All we deny in ourselves—whatever we perceive as

inferior, evil, or unacceptable—becomes part of the shadow. The personal shadow is the *disowned self*.

So what happens to all the parts of ourselves we sweep out of view? Whatever qualities we deny in ourselves, we see in others. In psychology, this is called projection. We project onto others anything we bury within us.

These psychological projections distort reality, creating a thick boundary between how we view ourselves and how we behave in reality. The shadow isn't a popular topic. Who enjoys owning their flaws, weaknesses, selfishness, nastiness, hate, and so on? Exploring our shadow side, however, gives us tremendous opportunities for growth and development.

✳

I like the way Robert Bly describes the shadow. He imagines it as a bag each one of us has been dragging behind us since we were children—a bag into which we stuff everything we don't want to be or think we shouldn't be. Maybe you have always had natural inclinations to lead, to create, to sing your specific song, but your power urges have felt wrong, unseemly, even shameful. So you pretend you don't have them. You put them in the bag. You present a different face to the world—more demure, less imposing. And then you envy or blame others for what you think you lack, when really it's trapped in your shadow bag.

Or maybe you think you must always be brave and tough. Into the bag go your uncertainties, your vulnerabilities, your tenderness, your longing for connection. On the outside you appear invulnerable, independent, a lone wolf. But that is not all of who you are. Or maybe you have unmetabolized wounds and grief, or anger, or repressed sexual desires, primal feelings, wildness. Better not show any of that. They go into the bag.

If you've been told since childhood that girls should always be "nice," your bag of shadows might contain the things about you that aren't "nice." If nice means always compliant and never contrary, into your bag go your firm beliefs, your big voice, your strong will, your ambition. If you were told as a child that girls who "want it" are sluts, your healthy sexuality gets stuffed in the bag, too. Some men stuff the same things that women do in their shadow bags. Some men stuff other things, especially if they were told as little boys "don't cry, be tough, man up, keep a stiff upper lip." Those men (and many women, too) drag behind them a bag packed with their sensitivity and emotional openness.

The energy of what we repress is strong. It can quite literally make us sick—in the heart, in the head, in the body, in the culture. Shadow material can leak out of the bag in unanticipated ways. Repress the natural human desire to shine bright, to influence, to create, and it seeps out as manipulation, or meanness, or resentment. Stuff in your shadow bag your sensitive nature, disown anything in yourself that society labels "weak" or "soft" or "feminine," and those repressed human qualities mutate and escape. They turn into the fear of intimacy, the compulsion to be right, all the way to misogyny and abusiveness.

This is why Jung encouraged people to bring the hidden parts of the self into the light, to understand them, to own them, to admit them, and to transform them. In the light, what is distorted is given the chance to heal and to return to its pure nature. In the light, we can take responsibility for the problems we often project onto others. Shadow work has been the most effective innervist work I have undertaken. It has often felt more courageous than the activist work I have done.

It's a lot easier to keep the repressed parts of who we are in the bag. It's less threatening to blame problems on someone or something else. But at some point, we may hear voices coming from our bag of shadows. Instead of ignoring them or drowning them out through work or drink or food or any of the brilliant avoidance strategies we may employ, shadow work asks us to turn around, open the bag, and examine what's in it.

I have my own term for shadow work. I call it *cleaning up my own bullshit*. Using plain language to describe psychological processes can demystify what may sound complex but what in reality is not rocket science. You can open your shadow bag and explore what's holding you back by asking yourself some questions. These are the questions I have asked myself about my shadow as it pertains to women and power: How much of my disempowerment at work is because I don't want people to think I'm powerful? Is it easier for me to play the victim than to come out of the power closet? Do I want to be liked more than I want to tell my truth? Is it less risky to blame others so that I don't have to take a stand for what I deserve? Am I willing to admit that I use indirect aggression and backdoor manipulation to get what I want? Am I willing to confront, as Jung said, "that which I do not want to be"?

It took me years to confront those questions and to determine what parts of my predicament were of my own making—my own bullshit—and therefore up to me to change, and what parts were structural in the work world and embedded in the culture at large. What parts would be best dealt with in a therapist's office, what parts in confrontations at work, what parts in the voting booth, the op-eds, the streets? I have never stopped asking these questions and benefiting from the answers I uncover within. I don't always get it right, but the point is to keep asking the questions.

Because I work with men, am married to a man, and am the mother of sons, some of the hardest shadow work I have done is looking honestly at some of the bullshitty ways I deal with men. Here's a shadow question I must continually grapple with: Am I asking men to be more vulnerable and communicative but still holding them to the old standards of manhood? I can't tell you how many times I have encouraged the men in my life to be sensitive, caring, and vulnerable, and then when those same men show signs of weakness or self-doubt or fear, I don't like it; I judge it. This isn't fair. It confuses the men who are trying to change; it messes with their heads (just like it messes with women's heads when men claim to support us in being whatever we want to be and going where we want to go, but then, when women are harassed or harmed, the message becomes, "You gotta be careful. Don't dress that way, don't say that, don't act that way, because boys will be boys.")

Research professor and author Brené Brown has been a frequent speaker at Omega. At one Women & Power conference she spoke about research sessions she was leading with groups of men on the subject of men, shame, and vulnerability. "I was not prepared," she said, "to hear over and over from men in these interview groups how the women—the mothers, sisters, girlfriends, wives—in their lives are constantly criticizing them for not being open and vulnerable and intimate. But when they do open up, when real vulnerability happens in men, those same women recoil with fear or disappointment, even disgust. After an interview with a small group of men, I was driving home and I realized that I recognized myself in that kind of behavior. And suddenly I thought, holy shit! I am the patriarchy."

Taking responsibility for the ways in which we collude with the old story of power—the ways in which we unwittingly keep the rules of patriarchal power alive—is just one example of shadow work. It takes courage to confront your own bullshit, but it is worth it, and it is a core component of doing power differently.

But wait a minute, you may be thinking. Why should women be the ones to do the shadow work? Won't my willingness to admit my faults be misconstrued as a weakness to be taken advantage of and a naive assumption that if I change others will want to as well? Haven't we been trying to be our best selves for too long? Feeling guilty when we fall short and apologizing for our imperfections? Haven't women been assuming responsibility for things that aren't even ours, covering for men, placating their egos, babysitting their emotions, even as they continue to benefit from their unfair advantage? Why should we do the hard work of transforming power before we've barely tasted empowerment at home and at work and in the world?

These are all worthy questions. It's a tricky subject, this idea of women looking within and taking responsibility for the ways in which we collude with the old power stories and the current rules of engagement. It may feel unfair and even dangerous for us to do so. This is especially true for women of color, lesbian and trans women, women who work in male-dominated industries, any woman within entrenched patriarchal family systems or controlling, abusive relationships. Even if a relationship isn't abusive, a reluctant, defensive partner can make shadow work risky business. That's when it's good to get help, to do the work in safe, supportive environments—therapist offices, couples counseling, groups of women dealing with similar issues. But I cannot speak highly enough of the importance of looking honestly at our full self, both the light and the dark, as difficult and disruptive as that may be. The truth is we can work on ourselves even as we stand our ground for justice and change. And I contend that doing both is more effective than doing just one.

The Jungian analyst Marion Woodman said, "Whenever we refuse to accept something as a part of us, we project that something onto others. A projection is like an arrow that flies out of your unconscious and finds its mark in someone out there. . . . Jung pointed out that our projections are like treasures that we believe other people have and that we want badly for ourselves. Withdrawing our projections lets us claim those treasures."

I want women to claim the treasure of our own power. I want us to stop believing that other powerful people have something special that we don't have. I want us to stop projecting onto men especially what "we want badly for ourselves," and instead to unearth our own brand of power, and then to partner with men to make the kinds of changes that will make life better for all people.

SCARS

The doors to the world of the wild Self
are few but precious.
If you have a deep scar, that is a door,
if you have an old, old story, that is a door. . . .
If you yearn for a deeper life, a full life,
a sane life, that is a door.

—CLARISSA PINKOLA ESTÉS

Nathaniel Hawthorne's *The Scarlet Letter* is number five on that list of the most-assigned books in American high schools I wrote about in Part I. The story is set in seventeenth-century Boston, Massachusetts, in a tightknit Puritan New England town. It begins as Hester Prynne—a beautiful young woman whom Hawthorne describes as resembling the Virgin Mary— is led from the town prison with her infant daughter in her arms and the scarlet letter "A" for adultery embroidered on her breast. The townspeople are abuzz with hearsay: Hester's husband has been lost at sea; she has had an affair and birthed a child out of wedlock. And if that isn't shameful enough, she freely admits her wickedness.

In the eyes of the Boston Puritans, Hester has committed an unforgivable sin—as grave as Eve's original sin. Not only has she broken the rules, but she also covers for the two men in her life, never revealing the identity of her husband who eventually returns to town, and keeping the name of her lover—who happens to be the church pastor—secret. As the story progresses, themes of sex and piety, vengeance and guilt, obedience and freedom swirl through Boston.

I don't know how teachers talk about the book today, but when I first read it in high school, I was led to believe that the moral of the story was this: that extramarital sex was a sin, that someone would pay, and that someone was usually a woman. I was confused about all of this in high school—confused and terrified. All around me girls were losing their virginity and keeping secrets from their parents. Yes, we were all more liberated than Hester Prynne had been, but we knew what would happen if we were caught. We'd be shamed, we'd be called sluts, we'd get pregnant. We would wear the scarlet letter.

I would have forgotten all about *The Scarlet Letter*, and certainly would never have reread it, if I hadn't gone through my own Hester Prynne experience—a messy divorce and the loneliness and insecurity of single motherhood. The night I revealed to my mother that I was getting divorced, she was horrified. She was concerned for me, and that touched me. But she seemed to be more concerned about what the people in her small town would say, and that infuriated me. I told her I didn't care what others thought (which was a lie). I told her that my husband and I had both betrayed each other, that the marriage had been dead for a long time, and that it wasn't a sin to want to be happy, to be loved, to be myself.

"You sound as shameless as Hester Prynne!" my mother exclaimed, as if Hester was her next-door neighbor.

"What do you mean?" I asked. "I don't remember that book."

"Read it," my mother said.

And so I went back and read it again. This time, I felt a kinship with Hester Prynne. I saw myself in parts of her story. When my mother and sisters were as deeply disapproving as the womenfolk of Boston, I was inspired by Hester's high-spirited independence. When I wore my sense of shame as if it were a scarlet letter on my chest, I noted how she wore hers with unabashed dignity. When I faced hostility and constraint at work, I dug deep and tried to find my place in what often felt like seventeenth-century Boston. And when single mother-hood seemed almost impossible to pull off, I turned to Hester. Despite her trauma she was a good mother and a fierce protec-tor of her daughter.

"You'll be scarred by this decision," my mother had warned. She was right about that. But like Hester Prynne, and like her scarlet letter, my scar would end up being the very thing that set me free. Years later, after my mother had died, and after I thought I had put the pain of the divorce behind me, I had an experience with a literal scar—a scar on my body—that shed light on my Hester Prynne phase of life and helped me put down the burdens of self-doubt and shame so many of us carry for far too long.

I was running a conference at Omega. Eve Ensler—the activist and playwright best known for *The Vagina Monologues*, and my partner in creating the early Women & Power conferences—was speaking. I came from backstage and took my place among hundreds of other women as Eve spoke about a scar on her body, how she got it, what it meant to her, and how she used its presence to remind her of the lessons she learned during a difficult time in her life. Then she asked us to close our eyes and think of a scar on our own bodies. To put our fingers on it and trace its contours as a way of remembering the stories embedded in our skin. How had it happened, Eve asked? What had we learned? What was the message in the tattoo?

My fingers went immediately to my thigh, to search for the barely palpable scar left by a wound from many years before. I slipped my hand under the waist of my pants and down the side of my leg until I found the spot. When I touched the raised piece of skin the story of my marriage and divorce came back to me, as if I was reading a book.

I saw myself at nineteen, a freshman in college. I was young for my age, innocent about love and sex, confused about who I was and who I wanted to be. I was seriously engaged in the anti-war and civil rights movements of the day, but I was also disturbed by the unexamined anger and violence creeping into the discourse and the demonstrations. I secretly wondered about the macho language, the mean-spirited aggression, and the ways in which the young guys leading the charge seemed similar to the men they reviled on the other side. How in the world would such an unpeaceful process ever produce peace? Was

I was really cut out to be an activist? These concerns burned within me, but I was reluctant to bring them up at meetings or with friends. They would only reveal my weak commitment to the cause, my lack of clarity and guts.

Instead, I began to read the words of Dr. Martin Luther King Jr. His assassination was still fresh in the American mind. Many of my friends had reacted to his murder with a surge of more radical activism. Others went in a different direction, attracted to King's philosophy of nonviolence. I was just becoming aware of those two forces at play within me—the justice seeker who wanted to fight the wrongs of the world and the wisdom seeker who wanted to own up to those same wrongs within my own heart, to change myself instead of trying to change others, to "be the peace," as Dr. King's mentor, Mahatma Gandhi, had said.

One day, in the spring of my freshman year, I joined a group of my activist friends who were illegally building a "people's park" on an empty lot owned by Columbia University. The park was a symbol of the students' fight against the university's plans to construct a new office building on the lot. For a few weeks, we'd been gathering and carting off trash—everything from discarded needles to a rat-infested couch. Now we were crowded into the bed of an old pickup truck, smushed between mounds of dirt, shovels, and other tools, on our way back from digging topsoil at a farm upstate. How we found a pickup truck in New York City, I do not remember.

What I do remember is this: as we bumped over the potholed streets of Harlem, it dawned on me that none of us well-meaning college students knew the people who lived by the vacant lot. Did they even want a park? Maybe they supported the university's plans. Maybe it was best to rid the neighborhood of that dangerous, drug-ridden plot of land. We had never asked.

I looked around at the kids riding in the truck with me—guys dressed in black jeans and leather jackets; girls with long hair and short skirts. I knew them all except for one guy. He had piercing brown eyes and auburn hair tied back in a blue bandanna. Who was he? I got the feeling he was different from the political types I had been hanging around with. I looked at him, and he looked at me. Something deep clicked. A few moments later, the truck stopped short. The tools, loose in the back, rattled around the truck bed. One of them—a pickax we had been using to whack through the rocky ground—slid fast into my leg.

The pain was so strong I cried out. The guy with the brown eyes came to my side. "Don't remove the ax," he said, taking my hand. "You'll lose a lot of blood."

"But it hurts!"

"Let me do it," he said. "I'm a medical student." I watched as his tapered fingers gently pulled the ax tip out of my leg. He took the bandanna from his hair and held it tight over the wound. Then he examined the ax. "I think a piece of metal chipped off and is still under the skin," he said. "You can come back to my apartment and I'll try to get it out."

"You must say that to all the girls," I said.

"No, just ones stabbed by pickaxes," he laughed.

And that was the beginning of our relationship. I did go back to his apartment. After trying to remove the metal shard he cleaned the wound and applied a Band-Aid. "I think I got it all," he said. I was impressed. But what impressed me even more was the round, black meditation cushion in the corner of his bedroom.

"What's that for?" I asked. I had never seen such a thing.

"It's a *zafu*," the medical student said. "A Zen meditation pillow."

I started meditating with him at a downtown Zen Center. We would ride the bus there, reading books to each other by Suzuki Roshi and Carlos Castaneda. We moved in together; we got married; we had kids and started Omega Institute. We made an excellent team: his vision, my creativity; his risk taking, my careful planning. His self-confidence and my need for his validation. All of this went into the making of our marriage and the organization we built together.

This is what I was remembering as I sat in the main hall at Omega, touching the scar, listening to Eve Ensler speak. "Ask the scar what lessons it holds for you," she said. I pressed on my leg. Images swirled up from the deep. I saw the good times and the struggles, the promises made and broken. What each of us brought to the other and what we withheld. The eventual break after fourteen years of a shared life.

I touched the scar again and remembered how during all the years of my marriage, the scar would become infected, swell, turn scarlet, and then heal and subside. And then one summer evening, right before our divorce came through, I was alone in my newly rented, rundown apartment. The kids were with my soon-to-be ex-husband for the night. I was brokenhearted for our children, lonely without them, scared I would not be able to pull off single motherhood. I was ashamed our marriage hadn't lasted, guilty about my part in its demise. I was unsure about work and terrified about my finances. Who was I without my husband? Could I steer the ship of my own life?

Suddenly, I felt the scar on my thigh tingle. I reached up the hem of my sundress, expecting to feel the telltale tenderness of infection, but this time, poking out of my skin, was a thin fragment of metal. I was stunned. "I think I got it all," he had said. Apparently not. At the end of our relationship the ax shard had freed itself. What did this mean?

And here I was now, in a conference hall years after the shard had worked its way out, sitting among hundreds of women, fingering my scar—my scarlet letter—still wondering what it meant. If strangers had walked into the hall, they would not have known what to make of the scene. We sat quietly, eyes closed, touching different parts of our bodies. Some women were crying, others were patting their scars and talking to themselves. I kept whispering to myself, "What does it mean? What does it mean?" All weekend I would put my hand on my thigh and wonder about that piece of metal and how it had entered my body at the very start of a relationship that would define the first half of my adult life and then exit when the marriage was ending.

The conference finished, but I was still thinking about the scar. As I drove home, I passed the entrance to the building where the kids and I lived right after the divorce—a big, dilapidated mansion built in the 1780s, later divided into apartments. My car almost drove itself up the long driveway. The place was even gloomier than I remembered. I thought back to the days when I lived there on the second floor with my little boys, overcome with guilt and fear, trying for their sake to pretend I was strong.

I parked, got out of the car, opened the big front door, and walked up the stairs. Standing outside the apartment door, the old feelings returned—the shame of having broken up a family, the guilt of dragging my kids through a mess of my own making. I touched my thigh and asked the scar, "Is this it? Is this the message? That I can let go of my guilt now?" But no, that didn't seem to be it. It was almost as if the scar was laughing at me: "You haven't let go of that stuff yet? Old guilt and shame? Come on, your kids are grown up; you gave them a strong foundation; they're fine."

Then what was it? What did it mean?

Then it came to me. Standing there at the top of the stairs in the dark hallway, I finally understood something important: Even though the ax shard was gone from body, my ex-husband was not. I still carried him around in me all these years later, still seeking his approval. We rarely saw each other; we were both remarried. On the surface we were long divorced. I had the legal papers to prove it and that sliver of metal from some other, mystical court of law. I had made great strides in finding and trusting my voice and using it at work and as a writer. But I was still driven by a need to be validated by someone outside of myself. Above all, by him. I still valued his opinions over my own, still sought legitimacy in his eyes—as if without his approval, my hard-won sense of self was meaningless. I kept him alive in me, a shard of hunger and anger. And it wasn't just him. That fragment of metal held within it the story of my childhood, and the stories of the ages—the stories that keep me from living, as Clarissa Pinkola Estés writes, "a deeper life, a full life, a sane life."

> The doors to the world of the wild Self
> are few but precious.
> If you have a deep scar, that is a door,
> if you have an old, old story, that is a door.
> If you yearn for a deeper life, a full life, a sane life, that
>   is a door.

I touched the scar again. Yes, it said. Yes. This. You can stop this now. This need to be seen by someone else in order to be real, to be valid. Your sense of worthiness was never your husband's to give. It was yours to claim, and yours to cherish, value, and trust. It's time to be your own source of dignity and power. Stop needing that from him. Stop blaming him for not giving it. Forgive yourself for taking a long, long time to get to this place. Forgive him for his part in the story. Free up all that wounded energy. Wear your scar as a badge of your growth and get on with your life.

I walked down the stairs and back to my car. As I drove home, I thought of all the women I had been with that day. I wondered what messages they had uncovered. I thought of women through the ages, the scars on their skin and the stories they carried. I thought of Hester Prynne and the red letter "A" she bore on her chest to the last page of *The Scarlet Letter*. I thought of how she transformed her years of guilt and punishment into compassion and empathy. How she cared for the sick and acted as a confessor to other women who defied Puritan norms. By the end of the book, many of the people in Boston who had reviled Hester saw her as an angel of mercy and were changed by her integrity and her ability to forgive. Hawthorne writes that the scarlet letter that had once stood for Adultery became "the symbol of her calling." He wrote, "Such helpfulness was found in her, so much power to do, and power to sympathize, that many people refused to interpret the scarlet A by its original signification. They said that it meant Able; so strong was Hester Prynne, with a woman's strength."

IN PRAISE
OF FATHERS

*Women are not going to be equal outside the home
until men are equal in it.*

—GLORIA STEINEM

I grew up in a house of women; I raised a house of boys. I loved being a girl. I love being a woman. And I have always loved being with women: as a daughter, sister, mother-in-law, friend, midwife, colleague.

I love boys, too—my sons, their friends, and now my grandsons. And I love men. I've married two of them (not simultaneously), and I have worked alongside men my whole life. I've often felt like an anthropologist in my own home, observing the behavior and customs of the other sex. At work it's been less like anthropology and more like a long trial by fire. That's where I finally identified my own style of power and the courage to speak my truth.

Most of what is written and researched about women and power is about the changing dynamics in leadership and the workplace. But the changes that blow my mind and excite me the most these days are the ones happening in the home.

Gloria Steinem has spoken at several Women & Power conferences. At one of them she brought along her new husband, David Bale, whom she had married just one year previously. The press had made a big deal of the fact that Gloria Steinem, the famous feminist who had often questioned the institution of marriage, had, at the age of sixty-six, finally married. When a reporter accused her of changing her tune, she said, "I didn't change, marriage changed. We spent thirty years in the United States changing the marriage laws. If I had married when I was supposed to get married, I would have lost my name, my legal residence, my credit rating, many of my civil rights. That's not true anymore. It's possible to make an equal marriage."

As we walked through the Omega campus, I asked Gloria what it was about David that had made her want to marry him. The first thing she said, before telling me about his career, or his work on environmental and animal rights issues, was that he had raised his four children as a devoted single father.

"He has the biggest heart of any man I've ever known," she said. "And the proof is in the way he raised his kids. That is what attracted me to him—his heart, his parenting, his priorities."

I told Gloria it was the same for me and shared with her the story of how I met my second husband. He had come to Omega to take a workshop led by the author Jean Shinoda Bolen, who had just published a book called *Goddesses in Every Woman*. He was the only man in the class of two hundred other participants. He told me he was trying to develop his "feminine side" because he had no training in the intimacy that being the primary parent of his five-year-old son required. I was intrigued. Here was a guy from Texas—a basketball jock and a businessman—who wanted to be a more nurturing father and a more emotionally available man. I found this sexy and appealing, and unusual.

Gloria's keynote speech that year centered around the division of labor in the home. She said, "Women are not going to be equal outside the home until men are equal in it. As long as working women also have to do the work of child and family care at home, they will have two jobs instead of one. Perhaps more important, children will grow up thinking that only women can be loving and nurturing, and men cannot. Achieving a society in which men raise children as much as women do is crucial."

That was in 2002. Since then, all over the world, in differing degrees of speed and completeness, I see men becoming equal partners in the home. I see the structure of the family evolving, the roles of mother and father expanding, and the division of labor changing, slowly, but changing, nonetheless. I've been waiting for these changes since I was a girl, concerned as I was about the gender imbalance in my childhood home. My dad was a man of his generation—the Greatest Generation, as it is called, because theirs was the one that grew up in the Depression and fought the Nazis in World War II. But theirs was also the generation of men who never talked about the war, never processed the trauma, kept that stiff upper lip that men were supposed to keep. Which my father did. He also kept his emotional distance from his four daughters. He was our provider and our disciplinarian, because that was what was expected of fathers in those days. He didn't do housework, didn't cook or shop, rarely played with us, didn't come to school functions, didn't know our friends. That was my mother's role (even though she worked outside of the home, too). Neither of them—true to the values of the Greatest Generation—talked to the other about their feelings regarding their family roles and gendered responsibilities.

My husband and I have been conducting a science experiment to attempt to reverse the imprinting we both received as kids. Here's the experiment: Take two people who were raised by Greatest Generation parents. Put them in the petri dish of what is called a blended family (a real misnomer, if you get the impression of a smoothie), give both of them busy careers, immerse them in a worldview of gender equality, and watch what happens.

Along with the happiness of finding a mate after difficult divorces for both of us, all sorts of subterranean issues began bubbling up and over the sides of the petri dish of our marriage—issues like unconscious male privilege and repressed, shadowy female anger. Issues like blame and shame, stress and frustration. But fortunately, we also added a few more ingredients that many in our generation (and even more in the generations that are following) have been fortunate to acquire: the commitment to listen and communicate, the courage to look at our shadows, and the desire to revise the roles we had inherited. And lo and behold, observe the daily miracles and blunders as the woman and the man take baby steps toward a different kind of marriage and homelife than their parents had.

My husband was raised in West Texas on a cattle ranch. He was a type-A 1950s American boy—an athlete and the valedictorian of his high school. He went to college on a basketball scholarship and then to law school. Sometimes I look at this guy who branded cattle and attended rodeos, and I think perhaps I have more in common with someone from another planet. I know he thinks the same way about me: a feminist from New York, a hippie in high school, a girl whose idea of competitive sports was a board game. But by the time we met, the crucible of divorce and single parenthood had made those differences less significant. We met on the shores of what I call being "broken open." Open to what? In my husband's case, open to the qualities he had not developed as a child or young man. He describes being a single father as a relentless master class in emotional intelligence. In my case, divorce and single parenting propelled me into self-reliance, decisiveness, and financial responsibility, aspects of my personhood that had been asleep within me, covered by cultural expectations, just as my husband's qualities had been untrained and dormant within him. We both had made some difficult changes from the inside out.

You may have heard this joke about inside-out change:

Q: How many psychiatrists does it take to change a lightbulb?
A: One. But the lightbulb has to *want* to change.

Human beings can change, but only if we want to, and only if we work at it. For the past one hundred plus years, women have been pushing hard for change. Why? Because we wanted to. We wanted to vote, we needed to work. We wanted to be safe in our homes and in the streets. To be strong in our bodies, to have our own voice. We wanted to dignify our true selves so we could make art, explore, invent, lead. We wanted to become educated in the ways of a world that had been denied to us. And we wanted to give birth to a different kind of world.

Now, both women *and* men have to want to change if we want to change the story—especially the story about who raises the children, who cares for the home, for the aging parents, for the emotional well-being of the community. To change that lightbulb, men in this century are going to have to want to change as much as women wanted to change in the last century. They will need to see that change not as a duty, but as a benefit that will bring good things to their lives and to all of life.

It may seem that the old roles are too deeply entrenched to make the kinds of changes I am suggesting here. But I'm an evolutionary optimist. There's a phenomenon in brain science called experience-dependent neuroplasticity. In plain English that means the brain learns from our experiences and actually changes its structure based on what information flows through it. This is how children learn, and now neuroscientists are proving that the brain remains plastic, pliable, throughout our lives. Research shows that even after a stroke or other trauma, the brain can reorganize itself, creating new neural pathways.

This is good news for changing the lightbulb. Deep neural grooves—also known as ancient belief systems—can be bypassed in even the most rigid of people and cultures, and new pathways, new ways of thinking, can be created. What I see happening now in the family lives and marriages of people gay and straight is proof of the ongoing evolution of the human species. I've had a front-row seat watching the ways in which the next generation—my children's generation—have been creating new neural pathways in the collective brain of our culture.

A few years ago, I was with my stepson and daughter-in-law at the birth of their first baby. During the labor, my stepson did everything he could to be involved, besides pushing the baby out himself. After the birth he used an app on his phone to help his wife get the hang of nursing. I'd hear his phone beep and then he'd say, "Honey, I think it's time to change to the left breast." He did the same with his second daughter, and since then he has been part of his children's lives in a way that is a living example of neuroplasticity. I don't mean to make this sound easy. It's not easy—not on fathers, mothers, relationships, children. The culture is not changing as fast as some families are. We need new neural pathways not only in individual men and women. The structure of the workplace and the priorities of the culture will have to change, too, but often big changes in the world start with those brave enough to make the changes in their own homes. As Gloria Steinem said, "Women are not going to be equal outside the home until men are equal in it."

My oldest son and his wife share the roles of breadwinner, homemaker, and parent. Being around them for me is a revelation—stereotype-busting, humbling, promising. From the moment my son became a father, he was as nurturing, attentive, and intuitive as any mother I had known. I once made the mistake of telling him, "You are such a good mommy."

My son responded, "I'm not a mommy. I'm a father. This is

what fathers do." Ever since then I have become so aware of the way society honors mothers and ignores fathers. Almost every magazine article or blog or book about parenting is addressed to mothers and celebrates mothers. From watching my son, I know now that fathers can, should, and do have what it takes to help raise our children. Deep inside we all have the capacity to nurture, sacrifice, teach, love—all the qualities we normally attribute to mothers. I'm on a crusade now to inject the word *father* whenever and wherever I find it excluded.

Recently, I was at my grandson's birthday party. I sat with one of the parents as he helped his three-year-old daughter recover from a tantrum while also changing his baby's diaper. His wife was mingling with the grown-ups outside on the deck. As this dad comforted his daughter, he reached into the diaper bag with one hand, held the squirming baby down with the other, and then with full confidence wiped the baby's butt and rediapered him.

"You know, what you are doing here is revolutionary," I said. The dad looked puzzled. So I explained: "Well, it may seem like all you're doing is changing a poopy diaper and calming a toddler, but I think it's as important as any social activist or artist or elected official who's trying to change the world. I actually believe that full-hearted fatherhood might save the world. At the very least, it will show your kids how to be a real man."

The young man looked up at me, smiled, and said, "This is just the way we roll. But thank you. Thank you for seeing what we're doing. Thank you for seeing what I am doing."

I admire the men who are changing in front of our eyes—

men who are swimming against the tides of the ages and becoming their full human selves. But I also must acknowledge that young man's wife out on the deck at the birthday party. She didn't ask her husband to change the baby's diaper. She expected it. She didn't apologize for being outside enjoying herself while he "babysat." Instead she believed in a man's capacity and right and responsibility to be an emotionally intelligent caretaker, just as he believes in her ability and right and responsibility to earn a living and express her full personhood.

I also have to give a shout-out to the same-sex couples who are redefining motherhood, fatherhood, and family life. Carlos Ball, author and professor of law at Rutgers University, writes this:

> My male partner and I nurture and care for our two sons in ways that are indistinguishable from what society has traditionally expected of mothers. We comfort our children when they get hurt, either physically or emotionally. We cook their meals and clean their room. We bake cupcakes for their birthdays and take them to their school so they can celebrate with their friends. We hug and kiss them as often as they allow us. We encourage them to explore their passions, not only for baseball and soccer, but for knitting and piano too. . . . It may be tempting to think that my partner and I mother our children because there is no female parent in our home. But we know heterosexual married men who do the same things for their children that we do for ours. . . . Much of society

continues to cling to the view that male parents are incapable of nurturing and caring for their children in ways that female parents do. The prevalent assumption is that mothers are more committed to parenting than are fathers. What we fail to recognize is that the idea that women are more capable inside of the home goes hand-in-hand with the notion that they are less capable outside of it. It should be as problematic to claim that women make better parents as it is to contend that men make better lawyers and doctors.

When my newest grandbaby was born, he landed in the neonatal intensive care unit (NICU) for a couple of days with breathing challenges. As my daughter-in-law recovered from a traumatic birth experience, my son camped out in the NICU and did not leave his baby's side. Late one night, before I left the hospital to get some sleep, I watched my son sitting close to the bassinet where his tiny son was hooked up to beeping and blinking machines. I listened to him singing to the baby. My heart swelled with pride. But it was when I noticed the baby's little hand curled around my son's finger that I was reduced to sobbing. I cried not only out of exhaustion and worry, but also in awe and appreciation for my son and his wife, and for all the men and women who are doing the gear-grinding work to undo centuries of imbalance.

As I fell into a fitful sleep I thought about how things are changing in the direction of freedom and equality at lightning speed for some women and some men in some parts of the world, yet across the globe, across the country, across town, unfair and often unfathomable gender norms for women and men are still upheld, using every means possible, from fear, to rape, to war. There are gulfs of inequity and imbalance everywhere, from the most egregious abuses to the general befuddlement that women and men experience in our work and home lives together. It will take generations to carve the deep and abiding changes—in our brains and in our cultures—we long for. It will take all of us to work for change in our own corner of the world, and never to forget those struggling for basic human rights, dignity, and safety.

DOING POWER DIFFERENTLY

I see the repression of the feminine principle
as the biggest problem on the planet,
and since the planet has become a global village,
power alone just isn't going to work anymore.
We will destroy ourselves.

—MARION WOODMAN

During the first Women & Power conferences, I'd get push-back on the use of the word *power*. I wasn't surprised. Many women in the audience and on the stage associated the word with ego, domination, and violence. Regardless of their age or race or the country they were from or the work they did, they were quick to say they didn't consider themselves powerful and they didn't want power.

For one of the conferences, we expanded the focus to the theme of women, power, and peace. Could women use the power we were finally gaining to promote peace in the world? We decided to invite all of the living women Nobel Peace Prize laureates to speak to that question. You might be thinking, Why would we want that many speakers at a conference? That's what I thought when we first had the idea—would we be able to afford and fit them all on the stage? Then I looked into it. At the time of that conference, only 16 of the 104 individuals ever awarded the Nobel Peace Prize had been women. Seven of those women were still alive. Two were not allowed by their home countries—Iran and Myanmar—to travel to the United States. That left only five women: Jody Williams from the United States; from Guatemala, Rigoberta Menchú; from Kenya, Wangari Maathai; and Betty Williams and Mairead Corrigan from Ireland. Corrigan was unable to attend, leaving only four. And still, it took considerable maneuvering to get those four women to a retreat center, down a little country lane in upstate New York, to discuss the topic of women, power, and peace.

The first night of the conference, Pat Mitchell, the renowned journalist who had been, among other things, the first female CEO and president of PBS, interviewed Jody Williams. Jody received the Nobel Peace Prize in 1997 for her work with the International Campaign to Ban Landmines. I could tell it was going to be a down-to-earth exchange when Jody came onto the stage barefoot, and Pat, in an act of solidarity, took off her shoes and tossed them backstage. The first question Pat asked Jody was about power—where hers came from, how she tapped into it, how she used it.

"Let's get something straight from the beginning," Jody said. "I don't like the word *power*. I don't consider myself powerful. I don't want power."

Pat was taken aback. "But you've gone into war zones," she said. "You've stood up to terrorists and tyrants. You've walked across minefields, probably barefoot, to call attention to the risks people face every day. You've mobilized teams around the world, and you won the Nobel Peace Prize for your efforts to ban landmines as weapons of war, but you don't consider yourself powerful?"

"No, I don't like that word *power*," Jody repeated. To her it stood for brute force and egomania. She said she didn't do what she did to win the prize for her own power but rather because it was the right thing to do.

Then Pat said something that I have returned to many times: "I don't think those urges are mutually exclusive, Jody," she said. "You're talking about the prevailing stereotype of power. But you can do the right thing and you can be powerful. Both can be true. All of us are seeking somewhere, somehow, to tap into that kind of power. Not the old kind of power, not power over someone else, but the power to change the reality of either our own lives or the lives of people around us. So, can we agree that there's a good power? There's nothing that feels better than tapping into that power. If you ever feel it, and you see a life or your community made better, that's a power you want to feel again."

But Jody wouldn't back down, which is probably how she ended up with a Nobel Peace Prize in the first place. She and Pat agreed to disagree. But for many of us, Pat's definition became our definition of power: power not in the service of brute force and egomania, not fueled by dangerous pride or violence, but "good power," the kind that is strong and potent and at the same time not self-aggrandizing, the kind that takes into account the feelings and contributions of others, the kind that can changes people's lives for the better.

As Jody and Pat talked, I looked around the conference hall and noted how much human ingenuity it had taken to get the word out and gather us all in one room—language and books and videos; cars and planes and cell phones—and I thought about the massive intelligence and imagination of our species. Why have we not applied that intelligence to changing the story of power—the way we get it, the way we share it or hoard it, use it or abuse it? When would Jody Williams feel comfortable using the word *power*?

I have spent years organizing conferences on these questions. I have steeped myself in the research on why women are generally the more empathetic of the genders; why when under stress, women, on average, "tend and befriend," while men more readily resort to strategies of "fight or flight" or "command and control"; why women more often show appreciation for the efforts of others, seek solutions to problems through communication; include rather than dominate. Why when girls and women are educated and empowered, the lives of the rest of the population also improve. And why when women assume leadership in families, companies, towns, and nations, issues like childcare, health care, and education all move to the front of the agenda.

There is plentiful research that demonstrates all of this— from social and brain scientists, corporate studies, and government statistics. But remember that research evidence is based on statistical averages. For example, research shows that men are taller than women. But there will always be some women who are taller than some men. So just as women in a variety of settings have been shown to be—for example—more empathic, there are certainly some men who are better empathizers than some women. But indeed, there have been enough studies done that reveal common denominators in women's instincts, behavior, and leadership.

I've studied the nature/nurture arguments, brain research, and feminist scholarship, all of which are fascinating and legitimate but together only prove the "both and" hypothesis about gender differences: both nature *and* nurture, brain structure *and* social conditioning, biology *and* society have contributed to the ways in which men and women are different from each other. But to be perfectly honest, it no longer really matters to me why, *on average*, women share certain ways of being, relating, communicating, and leading. I'm more interested in how women can proudly and loudly claim what dwells within us and move it out into a world starving for authentic female power.

Every time I hear myself say that phrase—authentic female power—a ping-pong game begins in my head. "Is there really a specific kind of female power?" I ask myself. "Yes, of course there is," I answer. "Just look at the research." "Yeah, but what about you-know-who in Congress, or that wacko on the local school board?" I ask. "I know, I know," I reply to myself, "but she's just a throwback." I tell myself that we are going to have to take the long view. That many of the first women to walk through the doors of power will end up playing by the old rules. Just getting into the old boy's network and staying there is hard enough. Making change while in there—even harder. The first women will open the doors for others, for women who want to do power differently.

That's what I tell myself. Sometimes I believe it, but then I think about my own lapses into the old kinds of power plays. And the ping-pong conversation continues back and forth across the net of my own mind. It's better to play ping-pong with another person, and so I brought this question about authentic female power to Pat Mitchell. If anyone has seen all sorts of people—women and men—in all sorts of power situations, it's Pat; she has interviewed hundreds of world leaders and business executives, and has worked for a variety of bosses and leaders, and has led teams of people at CNN and PBS and other organizations. I turn to her often when I need a reality check.

Pat listened patiently for a while, but then she interrupted. "You know what?" she said. "Can we stop asking that question about a female style of leadership? The research is *so* in. Ten, twenty years of studies done in business schools, in governments, in brain science. They all clearly show a distinct way in which women wield power. Sure, there are exceptions— for all sorts of historical and cultural reasons. But let's stop focusing on them. Let's stop questioning what we know is true. There are hundreds of empirical studies that codify women's ways of leading. We don't have to keep trotting out the data that show how our long exclusion from traditional power structures has forced us to do things differently: to be more collaborative much of the time, to be less prone to corruption, to instinctively move to fill the empathy deficit, to seek wiser solutions to conflict. Let's put aside the goal of doing it perfectly and replace it with the trust that we can do it differently."

Here's a list—culled from my research (especially from the work of Barbara Annis, CEO of the Gender Intelligence Group, and from Riane Eisler, author and cultural historian)— comparing how power has been brokered in the "old" ways to how women (and all people) are capable of doing power differently. Doing power differently doesn't mean throwing out every aspect of the old power paradigm. It's balance we're looking for. Neither column in this list is all good or all bad. I like the adage I learned from the philosopher Ken Wilber: "transcend and include." Transcend the destructive parts of the old story and include the parts that work well when combined with the long-neglected values women are more likely to draw on.

OLD-STORY POWER	DOING POWER DIFFERENTLY
Strong/weak hierarchy model	Partnership model
Authoritarian	Interactive
Collaborates competitively	Collaborates connectively
Values individualism, fortitude, and action	Values relationship, empathy, and communication
Withholds praise/ encouragement	Generous with praise and encouragement
Denies one's own mistakes and vulnerability	Transparent about mistakes and vulnerability
Dominates, interrupts, overrides	Listens, processes, includes

"Love is the real power," says Marion Woodman. "It's the energy that cherishes. The more you work with that energy, the more you will see how people respond naturally to it, and the more you will want to use it." Doing power differently is about fueling leadership with the energy of love. Women can do this; men can do this; everyone can do it. And what is the point of women claiming power if we don't show the way?

THE *FIRST*
FIRST RESPONDERS

The moment we start imagining a new world
and sharing it with one another through story
is the moment that new world may actually come.

—BRIT MARLING

If women are going to do power differently, we need art, novels, TV shows, and films to reflect our aspirations. Storytellers are the meaning makers in a society, and therefore they have a weighty influence and the ability to move humanity forward. Of course, sometimes stories are told just to entertain. There is certainly a time and place for that. But I feel a sense of loss when a book or a play or a film misses out on an opportunity to push the cultural dial, to change the narrative, to show and tell us how to do power differently.

In 2017, and then again in 2020, Wonder Woman reemerged on the big screen to join the pantheon of male superheroes who have become ubiquitous in cinema: Batman, Superman, Spider-Man, the Hulk, Green Lantern, Captain America, Thor, Wolverine, Iron Man, the X-Men, and a slew of other heroic stock characters. I know many people who love the Wonder Woman movies, especially women who had been waiting patiently for a female superhero protagonist. I appreciate that a woman director took the most powerful female comic-book hero and added her story to the genre. And I know that sometimes it is fortifying to experience a physical sense of "we can do it!" through a work of art. Still, I felt disappointed. I went into the first film expecting a new kind of power story. Instead, I left the theater wondering why the heck would a woman with superpowers choose to leave a tropical island paradise, pierce through the veil of time and space, just to go into a war and kick ass while looking hot?

Here are all the formidable superpowers Wonder Woman has (besides the ability to engage in combat in a strapless bustier): she has super-strength, bulletproof bracelets, and a Lasso of Truth. She's telepathic, clairvoyant, and can astrally project herself backward and forward through time. She can raise people from the dead, fly at terrific speeds, and is omni linguistic—speaking every language known to humankind. If you had those kinds of powers, wouldn't you use them to do something other than march into a World War I battle and do hand-to-hand combat? Just her command of many languages puts her at an advantage to sit everyone down and talk some sense into them, not to mention the ability to go back in time, raise some pertinent folks from the dead, and change what led up to the war in the first place.

But no, Wonder Woman used her superpowers to do power exactly the way it's always been done—to continue the fruitless pursuit of violence as a way to end violence; to perpetuate the narrative of winning versus losing. Some will say that she shows more empathy and remorse than other superheroes, but that hardly makes her a poster girl for doing power differently. Because what good is empathy or remorse if we don't actually change our basic behavior to match our elevated feelings? For millennia, women have honed the heart—empathy, intimacy, caretaking, communication—now it is time for us to validate what we know and to put it into action, into art, into education, into skills. But this is not what happens in *Wonder Woman*. Even on the all-female island where the movie franchise starts, the only power skill we see the girls and women being taught is warfare.

If I got to live on a tropical island with my friends who just happened to be magical goddesses, I don't think the only thing we would want to learn and teach is how to outmacho an adversary on the battlefield. I'd want to learn how to work through conflict before it turned into destructive behavior. That's really interesting to me, because it's something I could use some help with, something humanity has never been skilled at, something new and different, hopeful and possible.

Hell, if I had superpowers, I would leave that island only if I could strut onto the battlefield—I hope looking formidable and just a little hot—wave a wand, commence a weapons trade-in, heal everyone's wounds, feed them delicious food and wine, and forbid anyone to leave the table until we had hammered out how to share our resources in a just and equitable manner. I would use my powers to help the adversaries tame their childish egos and commit to living wisely and tenderly together, and to have fun while doing so; to be full of gratitude just for being alive on this precious little planet. Does that sound like magical thinking? Well, yeah! Wonder Woman *is* magic. She could have done whatever she wanted. She did not have to conform to the same old jacked-up hyper-masculine story line.

I hope as the Wonder Woman franchise evolves that we will see more sweeping and innovative changes to the story line. And while we wait for that, all of us can tell new kinds of hero myths. Mythmaking involves language, images, music, words, and sometimes only 140 characters. That's where we can start. Using words deliberately. Recently, I've been repurposing some well-worn phrases. For example, the phrase *first responder.* We've been hearing that phrase a lot recently, as brave men and women rush to those in need in fire and weather catastrophes, and in mass shootings and war zones. Their courage is worthy of our respect. But I've also been thinking about the people who work every day to avert catastrophes before they happen.

Let's call these heroes the *first* first responders. People who persist in difficult, often underpaid occupations and un-heralded volunteer positions that quietly serve and heal and educate. People like schoolteachers and social workers. Pro-fessionals like climate scientists or epidemiologists. I know these jobs don't sound particularly brawny or brave, but what if we exalted them along with the classic first responders? And what about day care providers and nurses and mediators? Isn't the work they do as valiant and necessary as the work of fire-fighters or police or soldiers?

Sometimes, when I introduce a friend, I'll say, "This is Linda, she's a first responder." And the other person will turn to Linda and say, "Oh, you're a firefighter?" I'll interrupt and say, "No, she teaches seventh grade. She's trying to save lives before they need to be saved. She teaches kids emotional intelligence skills like self-awareness and empathy and impulse control. She models how to ask for help, how to take responsibility and admit wrongdoing, how to value yourself so that you can love others. So yeah, she's a first responder—a *first* first responder."

Sometimes the other person's eyes glaze over. But I persevere.

When I introduce speakers at a women's conference, I often refer to them as *first* first responders. They may be teachers, economists, prison reformers, plumbers, artists, journalists, mediators, or meditators. I call them *first* first responders not because of their particular jobs but rather because of how they do those jobs—with old-style courage but also with kindness and connectivity. They have something else in common, too. They are not shy about telling their stories—and not just the pretty parts, or the successful parts, or the kick-ass parts. Sure, they tell those, but they also reveal their shadows, their stumbles, their learning curves. That's another quality of *first* first responders. They get their prideful ego out of the way. They tell the whole story.

I always make sure when I end a speech to remind people in the audience that they, too, have a story, and those stories are just as important as the tales being told on the stage. I encourage the audience to open up to one another over meals, in workshops, even in the bathroom (as women often do). To listen and talk about their work and the state of the nation and the world if they like, but, even more so, to talk about their families, their feelings, their grief, their joy, and the day-to-day intimacies and challenges of being human. Some may denounce that kind of talk as oversharing. That's a word I would like to banish. No one gets criticized for undersharing. No one says that word. I don't even know if there is such a word. There should be. Undersharing, underpraising, under–talking things out are at the core of some of humankind's deepest problems. I am on a mission to dignify the art of conversation, of chatting, of reaching across the table with a touch, of laughing and crying, of finding the value in each other's presence even if we disagree with each other's ideas. It's time for us to ignore the complaints that women talk too much, gossip too much, overshare, or whatever words are used to silence the ways in which women naturally connect.

I recoil not only at the word *oversharing* but also at words like *gossip*, *nag*, *busybody*, *tattletale*. So many of those words have been used to denigrate the tone of a woman's voice or the content of our conversations—to judge talking as an inferior function and to uphold the primacy of the "strong and silent" type. Who said that being strong and silent is better than being vulnerable and communicative? How about being all of that—sometimes strong, sometimes vulnerable; sometimes silent, sometimes willing and able to share, talk, commiserate, communicate?

The strong and silent archetype has been the prevailing image of the hero for so long that we don't question its supremacy. We don't wonder if perhaps there aren't other qualities a hero might add to his or her résumé—more relational ways of dealing with conflict and fear and chaos to balance out the sometimes appropriate, but greatly overused, response of strength and silence. We don't consider the costs to those who have been trained not to show weakness or vulnerability, not to talk or feel too much. It's just been part of the story forever. It's the theme song of patriarchy: "Strength is the backbone of power; silence keeps 'em guessing and reinforces the mystique. Strength and silence set you apart from the whiners and the oversharers."

To share your feelings openly, to give words to fear, to reveal that you aren't as sure of yourself as you may look—this is paramount to treason in the world of the strong and the silent. I grew up under the tutelage of a strong and silent type. I'm grateful to my father for teaching my sisters and me how to garner our strength, how not to be grumblers or quitters. He modeled forward movement, independence, and resourcefulness. But when it came to connecting, communicating, and showing us the soft side of his heart, he had no skills whatsoever.

I admired my father, and I felt sorry for him. Both. I sensed in his gruff exterior the blueprint for success in the world of men. But I also sensed that hidden in his silences were a little boy's hurt and a grown man's insecurities. There are many types of silences. In the forest, the quietude is ancient and deep; in the night sky, it is peaceful and vast. When my children would finally go to sleep and I would sit folding the laundry in the lamplight, the silence was a relief, medicine for the day's relentless noise and activity. The silence of a friend can be a way to show respect, care, or love when words won't suffice. In my father's silences, I sometimes felt the nobility of silence. Sometimes, when taking a hike with him or helping him mow the lawn, I would feel his quiet acceptance and appreciation, but mostly his silence was a warning: don't try to get any closer; I don't want your input; it's my way or the highway. It was a judgment: talk is cheap; it's mostly gossip; girls talk too much.

My father was a man of his generation. He was not supposed to speak his heart, ask for help, use words to reach across the ocean that separates one human from another. He was unschooled in the give-and-take of intimacy. I am sure that beneath my father's one-note strong and silent song was a rich symphony of feelings and experiences. But we never got to hear it. I know so little about my father's childhood, about growing up in the Great Depression, joining the army during World War II, marrying my mother, starting his career. I saw him shed a tear only once. I was a teenager, and quite uncharacteristically he told a story at the dinner table about getting into a fight in the army, sticking up for a Jewish friend who was being bullied by another recruit. His voice caught in his throat as he told the story. His eyes filled. He brought his hands up to cover his face. He had embarrassed himself in front of us, his family of women. I could feel his shame. I could feel the rage beneath the shame. He quickly stood up, rammed his chair against the table, and strode out of the house, slamming the door behind him. We were stunned. For once, the gaggle of girls around the table was silent.

We hear a lot about the shame women carry—about our bodies, our desires, our weight, our hidden stories of sexual abuse or harassment. But it's not only women who grapple with shame. Men sit on a powder keg of it: the shame they felt as little boys when they cried and were scolded because boys and men don't cry, or when they were made fun of for expressing love or fear—when they were told that boys and men keep those things to themselves. Beneath the refusal of men to apologize, or ask for directions, or admit to not having a solution, I contend there lurks the fear of being humiliated—by other men, and by women. I believe that much of men's aggression and violence are ways of covering that shame.

Charlie Donaldson, author, psychologist, and the founder of a men's resource center in Michigan, writes,

> Many men not only have been regularly shamed, but they also live in the incessant anxiety that they'll be further shamed. They live in fear of embarrassment, intimidation, humiliation. They are watchful, guarded, vigilant, they keep their distance, they act much more confident than they really are to avoid further shame. Men go through life as if they're on patrol in a war zone. If they are frequently ridiculed and mocked and bullied in their daily lives, they come to see the world as a deeply unsafe place . . . and sooner or later, some way, somehow, some time, many of them explode.

Often in my father's silence I could feel his anger just itching to ignite. So I steered clear of him, even though I felt a deep affinity with him and a longing to connect. I imagine he longed for that, too. But I could never figure out how to reach him. When I first entered therapy, I tried once or twice to cajole him into connecting more deeply with me. I was full of naive enthusiasm about the power of truth telling, convinced that all I needed to do was invite any other person, even my strong and silent father, to open up and he'd spill his heart . . . and we'd suddenly have a transformed relationship. Of course, that's not the way it works. It takes time and empathy and artistry to connect with anyone, and especially someone who had spent a lifetime building up his defenses and denigrating "girl talk."

The ways in which my father hid from his sensitive side were benign compared to other kinds of emotional suppression. He didn't drink. He was never violent. He was more of an escape artist. He took to the woods to escape what he didn't want to feel. I have a begrudging admiration for this strategy. He chose to escape before he exploded, which was a less harmful coping mechanism than what so many others turn to. It's not only men from my father's generation, or men in general, who have built up defenses against emotionality, connectivity, and vulnerability. Women, too, are conditioned to hide their feelings, especially if they are angry or shameful ones. Few of us receive education in how to be brave about our feelings, open to expressing them, and receptive to the feelings of others. Instead, we repress and implode, or we act out and explode.

When I led meditation and recovery classes for first responders after the 9/11 attacks in New York City, I learned just how terrified many men are to express themselves emotionally, to expand their "strong and silent" repertoire to include other ways of relating. Everyone in the class was a man who had been directly engaged in either firefighting or policing during and after the attacks. They had self-selected to take the class, and all expressed an interest in mindfulness meditation. I was moved by their willingness and by the discipline they showed in learning basic meditative stress-reduction techniques.

Sometimes in the quiet middle of our meditations a few of them would cry a little bit—I'd hear some stifled sobs or look up and see one of them wipe a tear from his eye. But when I encouraged them to talk about what they touched on during those meditation sessions, they'd shut down. Trying to get them to open up about what had happened in the dark stairways or on the chaotic streets was next to impossible. Here were these courageous firefighters and policemen who had put their lives on the line for others, but when it came to talking about their fear and grief, they seemed more scared to do that than to fight a fire or patrol a dangerous neighborhood.

I told them that the health of their relationships with their wives and kids depended on their willingness to open up. I told them their own health depended on it. I read them the research about how internalized grief, shame, and anger put men at greater risk for heart attacks, strokes, and other illnesses. I told them about the high suicide rates among first responders and war veterans and how those who can talk about their experiences are healthier, happier, and longer lived.

I even quoted Howard Stern, the New York City radio shock jock whom so many of the men in the group listened to every day. I read from an interview in the *New York Times*, where Stern talked about men and their emotions. "It's not that they have no emotions," he said. "It's that they are actually so emotional that somewhere along the line they had to close it off. That's a valuable technique for people who have been traumatized. I believe that traumatized people, and I include myself, learn how to turn off what you're calling a soul. It's not that they don't have one. It's that the pain of emotion is so intense they turn it off."

I told these 9/11 first responders that they had been traumatized. But not much I said seemed to make a difference. I appealed to them as fathers, sons, husbands. I talked about the undervalued power of emotional intelligence. I shared statistics about the role of repressed emotions and the lack of communication in domestic violence, divorce, addiction, suicide. One day, assuming the jocular tone that I had learned was the best way to engage with the guys, I asked, "Do you know what the number one risk factor for suicide is?"

"No, what?" one of the firefighters asked.

"Being male," I said. "Trying to outman each other. Trying not to look weak. Hiding your pain under your bro talk and other bullshit."

"Good try," the firefighter said. "But you're still not gonna get me to talk about my feelings or cry about how scared I was." He looked around the room. "We're not little girls. We're the strong and silent type," he said with pride. "You're not gonna get anything out of us, even if it kills us." The rest of the men laughed. But they also shrugged their shoulders and gave me apologetic looks. They knew their reluctance to open up was both funny and sad. They knew I was on their side; they understood the validity of the points I was making.

But when you have had it pounded into you since you were a child that strength and vulnerability cannot dwell in the same person, emotional intelligence sounds like a disease.

The biggest concession I got during that class series was when a firefighter agreed with me that talking about the attacks would probably help him. He was the one who came up with a phrase I like to use now as the companion to the strong and silent type.

"It would probably help the whole world if men could open up a little," he told me at a break so that the other guys wouldn't hear him. "I get what you are saying about other ways to be strong, other ways to show courage. Not always strong and silent. Maybe brave and open would be a good alternative."

"I like that," I said. "Brave and open. The brave and open type."

"You know," he said, leaning closer to me and speaking almost in a whisper, "there's a good chance that 9/11 would never have happened if those idiots who flew their planes into our buildings could have talked things out. But they didn't. And even though I hate them, I understand them. They were probably strong and silent types, too."

I told him that a brave and open type would share that tidbit of wisdom with the rest of the group. He said he'd try. So after the break he mumbled some words about it being true that it's probably good to talk things out, that his wife tells him that all the time, and that it might even be a good thing for the state of the world. Then he said, "Like Robin Williams says, 'If women ran the world, we wouldn't have wars, just intense negotiations every twenty-eight days.'"

Everyone laughed. I laughed. "That's a sexist joke," I said, "but my biggest problem with it is that it's inaccurate. If women ran the world, we'd be talking every day, all day long."

The men groaned.

"I'm serious," I said. "If we ran the world, you all would have to go to training programs that taught you how to open your hearts and your mouths at the same time. And you'd be better off for it. So would everyone else."

A couple of years ago I got a handwritten note in the mail from that firefighter. He wrote:

You probably think I wasn't listening to a word you said but I was. I have continued to meditate since I took that class with you. It has helped me. And I remember how you talked about the cost of being strong and silent all the time and how it was brave to open up. After one divorce, one heart attack, and a bout of depression, I am beginning to understand what you meant. I am much more open now with my new wife. I talk more and I listen more. I am a better husband and father because of that. I'm a better partner at the station. And I think that's pretty darn brave and open of me. Some of the guys roll their eyes when I talk about being brave and open. I tell them that their anger and their bullshit are just covering up their pain. They tell me to shut the f up. But I think they may be listening like I did.

Love, Bill

PS: I actually do believe women should run the world.

VIVERE MILITARE EST

*Violence is immoral because it thrives
on hatred rather than love . . .
violence ends up defeating itself.
It creates bitterness in the survivors
and brutality in the destroyers.*

—DR. MARTIN LUTHER KING JR.

It was totally predictable that when women began to strain against the old stories, many of the men in their lives would feel threatened—psychologically, financially, sexually. This has been so since the beginning; when women claimed autonomy and agency, demanded decision-making control, made money, and made changes to the status quo, men took it as a threat not only to their control but also to themselves, to the core of their masculinity. It was true then, and it is still true. And therefore, especially in societies where male power is held in place by strict moral codes and enforced by violence, it is naive not to expect backlash, blowback, scapegoating.

Still, I am shocked by the rationalizations some otherwise

smart men revert to in order to keep women unequal, off-balance, out of power. Just go online to the many sites about men's rights, masculinity, or dating if you would like a quick reminder of the persistence of the patriarchal mind-set. I recommend to anyone who thinks we have moved past the old attitudes toward women to search the internet for phrases like "men's rights" or "the feminization of culture" and to listen to the podcasts and to read the articles and especially the comments. When I do the same, I find myself talking back, as if in debate with the authors.

I did this the other day after reading an interview with the renowned journalist and adventurer Sebastian Junger, about the anxiety men are feeling as "gender-specific" jobs disappear. Junger spoke longingly of the old days when men could be men at work and at war, when society needed the very things men are equipped to do. He spoke about how war is an eternal human experience and that men are biologically inclined toward warriorship—"Wired for war" are his words. "The male response to war," he said, "is an evolutionary adaptation that clearly works for our species."

"How exactly has that worked for our species?" I countered. I was alone in the house, so I spoke out loud in dialogue with Sebastian Junger. "War in the twenty-first century is bringing us to the edge of extinction," I said to the imaginary Mr. Junger. "If nuclear weapons don't destroy the earth, then the ungodly misdirection of resources will. Every dollar spent on war, every young person lost, every city and country destroyed, every technological innovation applied to the military, could be used in favor of life as opposed to death and destruction. War is a lack of imagination in a time of great peril."

Imaginary Sebastian Junger repeated, "But men are wired for war."

"Well," I continued, "if you think that men are wired for war, and women are wired for caretaking, then wouldn't it be better to put women in charge? How about giving women a chance to lead humanity out of the never-ending cycle of war and destruction? This is not a vote against men. This is a vote for doing power differently."

The argument continued with Junger explaining to me that war serves as one of the only remaining rites of passage for young men, a way for them to find out who they are, to bond with their brothers, and to feel heroic, all of which are important to the male psyche. And me questioning the wisdom of settling for such a limited worldview.

Brett McKay, the founder of *The Art of Manliness*, the largest independent men's interest magazine on the web, echoes Junger's beliefs. McKay writes,

> Fighting and violence are at the very core of masculinity. Researchers theorize that nearly every part of uniquely male physiology—from our shoulders, to our height, to our faces and hands—evolved expressly for the purpose of man-to-man combat. Yet few male propensities have been as maligned. . . . Just like masculinity as a whole, violence itself is thought to be the problem, rather

than how violence is used. When we think about male violence, we think about rape and domestic battery. We don't think about all the violence that's done on our behalf so we can live our safe, comfortable existence where we never have to see two men grapple for their lives. The outsourcing and distancing of ourselves from violence has led to the naive belief that it is possible and desirable to try to breed this trait out of men altogether. Instead of teaching young men: "You've got an amazing power and energy inside of you—a force that drove the Vikings and the Spartans and the Minutemen and the GIs," we teach them: "You have something wrong with you, a dark, bad drive that hurts people. Deny it. Smother it. Exclaim that you're not like other men and reject it altogether!"

Here's what I would like to say to McKay: "Violence *is* a dark, bad drive that hurts people! Let's help men find other ways of expressing anger and rage and the urge to protect." But I know what his comeback would be. Exactly what he wrote in a blogpost online:

Nobody likes violence until they're sitting on a plane that's been hijacked by terrorists and it's the men who hatch a plan to take it back and kill them. Nobody likes violence until someone breaks into their house, and a man gets up to confront the intruder. Nobody likes violence until their freedom is at stake and they need men to storm the beaches of Normandy and run a knife through the enemy's kidneys. . . . *Vivere militare est*—to live is to fight.

"But Brett," I say (and Sebastian, and all the other writers and thinkers who lean in this direction of equating masculinity with violence), "as long as we use violence to combat violence we will live by that credo: *Vivere miliatre est*. And as long as the story line that guides humanity is 'to live is to fight,' the world order is seriously endangered, and stacked against those who subscribe to a different set of values."

I bring this same argument to the writer and thinker who peeves me the most—the Canadian university professor Jordan Peterson. Peterson is an erudite scholar, deeply schooled in mythology, religion, and psychology, and also a bombastic critic of the "feminization" of culture. He is a bestselling author and has a huge online following, mostly of young men who watch his YouTube lectures and relate to his contention that "the masculine spirit is under assault" as society is becoming "feminized."

What does Jordan Peterson mean by "feminized"? Women, he says, are "agreeable and conscientious." Men are aggressive, competitive, and tough. From the beginning of time, says Peterson, leaders have needed to be aggressive, competitive, and tough. Therefore, using what he seems to think is his genius for deductive reasoning, men are made for leadership and women are made for the agreeable and conscientious realms of the home and the kindergarten classroom.

I actually wrote Jordan Peterson a long email debating this illogical logic. This is part of what I wrote:

Dear Jordan Peterson,

I would like to preface this letter by saying that what you call the feminization of our culture, I call its re-balancing. I am not clamoring for a female-run world. I am only stating that the world is out of balance after millennia of male-dominated leadership. Of course, humankind would be suffering from other problems if throughout history men and their talents had been relegated to a small sphere; if their sensibilities had been ignored and denigrated; if their bodies had been routinely violated; and if their creativity, intellect, and leadership had been suppressed. If women's ideas, symbols, and metaphors had dominated in shaping our common history, humanity would have missed out on the great genius of the male of our species. Instead, it was women who were excluded. And in doing so, we have not only lost the genius of the female perspective, we have also suffered from an excess of the masculine, and we have prohibited both women and men from discovering their own inner balance, their full humanness.

But what if there had been gender balance in the family, in education, in the arts, and in the halls of power? Not only an equal ratio of women to men, but also an equal valuing of women as unique individuals, and as a group? What if women's concerns, challenges, and experiences from girlhood to old age had informed life for everyone? What if "feminine" values and "masculine" values had both infused art and religion? What if women's voices had chimed in equally when the big questions were asked and answered: How should limited resources be shared and economies constructed? What should be done when conflict and evil emerge? What work is important and how should the division of labor be fairly organized? How can we find ways of increasing joy and diminishing suffering for all who share the Earth?

You contend that women are wired to be agreeable and conscientious. And that men are naturally aggressive and tough. Well then, why can't the core competencies of a leader include agreeableness and conscientiousness, as well as aggressiveness and toughness? Does it have to be an either/or equation? Wouldn't a combination of those qualities make for a better society? If our leaders were expected to develop missing aspects of their full humanity wouldn't that make for better relationships, less violence, and a more naturally leveled playing field? Leadership values were prescribed by the first leaders, who were men, because of both nature and nurture. But values are not set in stone. They have changed throughout human history, and will continue to change, and that's a good thing.

For the past 100 years women have chosen to move beyond typecasting. We have taught ourselves how to be more assertive, how to strategize, how to negotiate, how to be more aggressive when necessary and how to bring our agreeable, conscientious traits along with us into the workplace, into leadership, into arenas we had never entered before. Isn't it possible for men to do the same—to keep the best of their masculine traits while also learning new skills and developing different qualities that will allow them to be hands-on fathers, caretakers of older parents, emotionally intelligent members of families and groups? Isn't it possible for men to stop worrying about whether these traits are emasculating or shameful? Girls feel a sense of pride if they are called tomboys; women feel accomplished when they join the ranks of male endeavors. Can boys be raised to feel pride when they exhibit more "feminine" qualities? And if not, why not? Why is a "tomboy" exalted, but a "sissy" is a source of shame? Why do men scorn the "feminization" of culture? What does this say about men's deeper feelings about the value and treatment of women?

Mr. Peterson, I have heard you say that we must adhere to the traditions as put forth in the old myths and stories, but people made up those stories, and people can change them. The basic belief of feminism is not that women are right and men are wrong. It is merely that women are people and therefore their voices matter, their values matter, and their stories matter. It's time for women to tell their versions of what it means to be fully human; it is time for men to respect those insights; and it is time for all of us to integrate them into a new story of power.

I'm still waiting for Dr. Peterson's response.

A DAY
WITHOUT
A WAR
METAPHOR

Speech has power. Words do not fade.
What starts out as a sound, ends in a deed.

—ABRAHAM JOSHUA HESCHEL

Two months after the 9/11 attacks on the World Trade Center, I was at an airport, waiting on what has now become the ubiquitous long security line. I was behind a mother and her two-year-old child. As we waited, slowly pushing our bags forward, the little boy was in his stroller, happily eating a snack; ten minutes later he was playing with a toy; as we moved closer to the security gate, he began to squirm in his seat, demanding to get out. By the time we got to the checkpoint, the little guy was having a tantrum in his mother's arms. I offered to hold the boy so the mom could gather their bags and fold up the stroller. She gratefully accepted. As I took the child, I said to the mother, "Two-year-olds are like time bombs, aren't they? You just never know when they're going to explode."

A few minutes later, seemingly out of nowhere, a security official rushed over to me, grabbed the boy, and gave him back to his mother.

"Come with me, please," the official said.

"Why?" I was stunned.

"Just please come with me, ma'am." He picked up my bag and motioned for me to follow him into a little office behind a glass wall. Once there, another man opened my carry-on and began examining its contents.

"Do you know why I have you in here?" the man asked.

"No, I do not."

"A traveler in your line heard you say 'time bomb.' Are you carrying an explosive device?"

"Of course not," I laughed.

"This isn't funny, ma'am."

"I was referring to the two-year-old," I said. "You know how little kids just go off when you least ex—"

"We will need to search your body for any remnants of explosive material," the man interrupted. "Please wait here for a female agent."

After a search and some more questioning I was released, but the experience made a lasting impression on me. I never again used a war metaphor in an airport. I also began paying attention to the common usage of words and metaphors derived from war. We describe almost everything we do—from having a discussion to having sex, from winning to losing, starting or ending, helping or hindering—using the words of combat, force, explosions. We call an argument a battle, and cooperation a truce or a cease-fire. In conversations about all sorts of mundane things we talk about bombardment, firestorms, front lines, and wars on everything from drugs to the middle class. We join the ranks, take it to the mat, get in the cross fire, call in the troops. These words seep into our consciousness and affect the way we go about our daily lives and work projects and intimate relationships.

I'm not suggesting we police people's language. It's so annoying when we do that to each other. What I am suggesting is becoming aware of the words we use, choosing them deliberately, and noticing how that changes our perspective. For example, imagine if we talked about scientists working in the kitchen of cancer research as opposed to them working on the front lines. No longer are the scientists in a battle against cancer, or in mortal competition with other scientists, but instead they are in the kitchen, cooking up recipes that nourish and heal. There's absolutely no reason why "kitchen" isn't as legitimate a metaphor as a regiment's "front line," since most people spend more time at home in their kitchen than at war on a battlefield.

The next time you find yourself using metaphors from violent confrontations—either in warfare or contact sports—play around with other ways of describing common situations. There are so many other words we could use to describe a woman's beauty other than "bombshell" or "knockout," or a person's power other than "heavy hitter," or a plan's failure as a "dud." And pay attention to how often you use sports idioms like "curve ball," "full court press," "slam dunk," "low blow," "on the ropes," "roll with the punches," "saved by the bell," "under the wire," "throw in the towel," "hands down," "dead ringer," or "down to the wire," to name just a few. Maybe it's a perfect expression for what you mean. Fine. But maybe you want to look for other metaphors from other pursuits besides war or sports. Just to balance things out, just to fill our imaginations with the full range of what it means to be human.

After my "time bomb" experience at the airport, I did an experiment and tried to go a day without using an aggressive metaphor. I did this not because it is always wrong to use those kinds of words—they describe aspects of the human experience, but they do not describe the whole of it, and in overusing them we give power to the deeds they describe. At first, I had to look up some phrases I heard myself say. Where does "powder keg" come from? What *is* a "low blow"? Why do we call an authentic person a "straight shooter"? And what the heck does "no-holds-barred" refer to? That one surprised me. I had used it in a sentence describing what I felt for my newborn grandson. "I just love him, no-holds-barred," I told a friend. Hmmm, what kind of metaphor is that, I wondered. I assumed it was a sports saying that meant relaxing all the rules of the game. But I didn't know that the "holds" in this phrase refer to wrestling moves.

There was a time in the sport of wrestling, going all the way back to ancient Greece, when there were no formal regulations. You could do whatever you wanted to an opponent in order to win the match. Here's the earliest reference—from an 1802 newspaper article—that I could dig up. ("Dig up." Hooray, a farming metaphor!)

"Wm. Gibbs, the Kansas man, and Dennis Gallagher, of Buffalo, engaged in a wrestling match at the opera house here tonight. Gibbs was strangled into insensibility and may die. The conditions of the match were best two in three falls Greco-Roman style; no holds barred."

Once I knew the origin of "no-holds-barred," I decided to stop using it. Why would I use a violent wrestling metaphor to describe my love for a baby? Why would I use it to describe most of the things I did on a daily basis? On the one hand, boycotting (or girlcotting, as my husband suggested I use) one metaphor wasn't going to move the dial of social change all that much, but it did have the effect of reminding me of the imbalanced roots of our language. As I searched for other words to use, I realized how potent speech can be.

Rabbi Abraham Joshua Heschel wrote, "Speech has power. Words do not fade. What starts out as a sound, ends in a deed." Heschel loved language. He knew its power. Born in Poland and educated in Germany, he witnessed the rise of the Nazis and their use of words to motivate and agitate. His mother and sisters were murdered in bombings and concentration camps. He escaped a similar fate, immigrating to the United States in 1940. From then on, he used his words carefully and magnificently to further human rights. His speeches and books and poetry are clothed in kindness and justice and beauty.

As I replaced aggressive metaphors with more nurturing ones, I realized that our vernacular reflects a cultural fear of tenderness—as if anything sounding sentimental emasculates the language. When I gave my first TED talk, I had to speak right after one of the best talks I had ever heard anywhere (and because of my work, I have been privy to a prodigious number of speeches). Giving a TED talk, perhaps because the speakers know if they do a good job their message could reach millions of viewers online, is a nerve-wracking endeavor. As I waited to give my talk, I was in the greenroom with the speaker who would go onstage right before me and the one who would follow. The man preceding me looked like a pro football player and spoke with a soft and warm voice. He introduced himself: Tony Porter, the cofounder of A Call to Men, an organization that believes ending violence against women starts by redefining what it means to be a man. The person who would follow me was Madeline Albright, the first female secretary of state in US history. She admitted to Tony and me that she was nervous, and I commented that I was sure she had done way more intimidating things in her career than give a TED talk. All three of us laughed. We were all nervous.

I still get PTSD just thinking about watching Tony Porter speak and receive the first and only standing ovation of the day, knowing that I would have to go next. In his talk, Tony challenged the limiting definition of manhood, which he defines as the "man box," and the ways in which sensitivity and tenderness are socialized out of boys and men. It's in the man box, he says, where men learn not to ask for help, to act like they have everything under control, to resist appearing vulnerable even if it affects their physical wellness, mental health, and emotional relationships. At the end the talk, Tony said something I have never forgotten:

> I can remember speaking to a 12-year-old boy, a football player. And I asked him, I said, "How would you feel if in front of all the players, your coach said you were playing like a girl?" Now I expected him to say something like, I'd be sad; I'd be mad; I'd be angry, or something like that. No, the boy said to me . . . "It would destroy me." And I said to myself, God, if it would destroy him to be called a girl, what are we then teaching him about girls?

This is such an important question. What are we still teaching boys and girls about their self-worth? Why would a boy be destroyed if he was told he was "playing like a girl," when a girl would feel pride to be told she was "playing like a boy"? Why do the words *playing like a boy* carry with them the air of vigor and strength, yet the words *playing like a girl* indicate weakness, deficiency?

Maybe you know a little girl who loves to play sports or wander around in the woods in dirty jeans, or a little boy who enjoys playing with dolls or spending the day curled up on the couch reading a novel. Do a word experiment right now: Think of that little boy and say, "He's a sissy." Now, think of the little girl and say, "She's a tomboy." What do you feel about the boy? About the girl? Find a word other than *sissy* to describe the boy so that his unique self is validated and celebrated. Find a word other than *tomboy* to describe the girl, so that her adventurous spirit is not associated with being boy-like, but rather just being herself.

Here are some other phrases to play around with. Say them out loud and reflect on how you feel as you speak each one.

He's a mama's boy.

She's daddy's little girl.

It's an action film.

It's a chick flick.

He's very rational.

She's very emotional.

Or flip that last one and say:

She's very rational.

He's very emotional.

Every time I hear a strong, opinionated girl or woman described as bossy or bitchy or intense, I interrupt and suggest other words, like smart, powerful, brave, or, as Toni Morrison described herself, *gallant*. When a woman cries at work, or when a man asks for help, admits his fears, shares his heart, I like to acknowledge that kind of emotional intelligence as risky and courageous. Substituting one word for another may seem inconsequential, but words shape people and cultures, and "what starts out as a sound, ends as a deed." (In Part III, I explore some ways of flipping scripts, substituting language, and being inventive in daily speech.)

When it no longer would destroy a boy to be likened to a girl, when a girl feels vital doing the things she values, when it's considered as brave to be "womanly" as it is to be "manly," then boys and girls, men and women, can break out of the boxes that constrain us all. Tony Porter ended his TED talk like this: "I remember asking a nine-year-old boy, 'What would life be like for you, if you didn't have to adhere to this man box?' He said to me, 'I would be free.'"

I use the words of the historian Gerda Lerner at the very start of this book. "What will the writing of history be like," she asks, "when the definition is shared equally by men and women? Will we devalue the past, overthrow the categories, supplant order with chaos? No—we will simply step out under the free sky." This is what that wise nine-year-old-boy meant when he answered Tony's question about leaving the man box. This is what happens when, in Gerda Lerner's words, we "describe the earth and its workings in male and female voices," and when we choose words that value the male and female experience equally. "We now know," Gerda writes, "that man is not the measure of that which is human, but men and women are. This insight will transform consciousness as decisively as Copernicus' discovery that the earth is not the center of the universe."

The Copernican Revolution, as Copernicus's theory of the universe is now called, was a paradigm shift away from a worldview that Western cultures had adhered to for more than a thousand years. His idea—that the Earth revolves around the sun and therefore is not the center of the universe—was deemed heretical by the Catholic Church. For a century following Copernicus's death, only a handful of astronomers in all of Europe were brave enough to uphold and further his work. Galileo was one of them. He was placed under house arrest for the latter part of his life after the pope declared him a heretic for "having believed and held the doctrine (which is false and contrary to the Holy and Divine Scriptures) that the sun is the center of the world, and that it does not move from east to west, and that the earth does move, and is not the center of the world." It took more than three hundred years for the church to clear Galileo's name.

The word *revolution* has come to mean a sudden and often violent overthrowing of those in political power. But not all revolutions are violent. In fact, the word *revolution* stems from the Latin *revolvere*, which refers to the heavenly bodies making their slow and steady progress through the sky. Women are at the forefront of that kind of revolution now—a paradigm shift away from a gendered value system where the male experience is at the center of reality and all other ways of being, thinking, feeling, and doing are at the periphery. Like in Copernicus's and Galileo's times—and like in any time when cherished and long-held beliefs and ideas are being challenged—this revolution of values requires a blend of audacity and patience, courage and endurance.

A REVOLUTION OF VALUES

*I see the repression of the feminine principle
as the biggest problem on the planet,
and since the planet has become a global village,
power alone just isn't going to work anymore.
We will destroy ourselves.*

—MARION WOODMAN

I still get the Sunday *New York Times* delivered to the top of my driveway. I like the ritual of retrieving it, and then the physical act of turning the pages of a newspaper as I drink my coffee. I like hearing the paper crinkle; I like discovering articles I may never have seen by browsing online. I like choosing which section to peruse first. Sometimes it's the Style section to read about the marriage of the week, or the Real Estate section, because I'm a voyeur of other people's houses. Or it might be the Travel section because, even though I'm a homebody, I still want to know the terrain in case I ever get it together to visit Estonia or the Seychelles Islands.

But what I like to read most are the Sunday letters to the

editor. I want to see if other readers were bothered or cheered by the same things I was all week. I find other peoples' opinions enlightening, especially when they are different from mine, or broader, or more creative. I'm less likely to take the words of one journalist as gospel if I also listen to the voices of the whole village.

Recently a woman, a history PhD student named Kimberly Probolus, wrote to the *Times* complaining that the letters to the editor "skew male." She began her letter with these lines: "In 1855, Nathaniel Hawthorne wrote to his publisher, 'America is now wholly given over to a damned mob of scribbling women.'" Ms. Probolus noted that Hawthorne's letter expressed the belief that "women's writing was not worth reading or publishing, that their words and ideas didn't matter, and that their work was, to use the language of Hawthorne, 'trash.'"

"As I scan through various national newspapers," Ms. Probolus wrote, "day after day, year after year, I find myself hoping that someday, eventually, women will be represented proportionally. I am always disappointed; they always skew male. Perhaps Hawthorne's disdain for scribbling women is not such distant history."

Like me, Probolus loves the letters to the editor in the *Times*. She calls it "the most democratic section of the paper because children and adults, billionaire philanthropists and minimum-wage workers, and people of all genders can contribute. Each has an equal opportunity to express her or his thoughts and participate in a robust debate in the public sphere. Therefore,

I'm troubled that in 2019, the *New York Times* struggles to find women's letters that are worthy of publication."

The next week, the *Times* editors responded with a letter titled "We Hear You." "Ms. Probolus is right," they said. "Even before we received her note, we'd wrestled with the fact that women have long been underrepresented on the letters page. By our rough estimate, women account for a quarter to a third of submissions—although women do tend to write in greater numbers about issues like education, health, gender and children." They noted that the lack of women's voices is an "industry-wide phenomenon," and they were going to address it by deliberately choosing more letters from women.

I was disappointed by their response but glad to have such a clear example of the lack of bold imagination in addressing this "industry-wide phenomenon." It's the same lack of imagination I see everywhere in the ways we are dealing with gender inequality. Yes, an important and logical first step is to add more women's voices into the conversation, but that won't get to the roots of the "phenomenon."

Here's a way to get closer to the roots, a solution that is far more revolutionary than merely adding a dollop of females into the same old recipe: If women already write to the paper more frequently when the articles are about "education, health, gender and children," and if it's important to the *Times* to hear more from their women readers, why then not report more— and more seriously—on subjects women care about? Why not move stories about education, health, gender, and children to the front page? Why not spend more of their resources researching these issues, dignifying their importance, embedding reporters at the front lines of schools, hospitals, and other everyday landscapes of human life and activity? Why not write about these places and the stories within them with the same kind of gravity that the news media gives election scandals, violent crime, and war? Why relegate to the Style section stories about human relationships, parenting, mental health, love, and connection? What do those issues have to do with "style" anyway?

As long as what has always qualified as "the news" is determined by an uncontested value system, only certain types of people will find themselves represented in the big stories. By creating a closed loop of interest begetting content, and content begetting interest, men will continue to be the ones commenting on stories. "We are sensitive to gender imbalance," writes the *Times* editors at the end of their letter, "and as editors of a space dedicated to readers' voices, we are determined to have it reflect more closely society as a whole. . . . But we need your help. So we want to urge women—and anyone else who feels underrepresented—to write in." Except women— "and anyone else who feels underrepresented"—will not be more likely to write in if the articles don't reflect the fullness of what they care about, what they value, what they experience.

A Pew Report ranked the subject areas covered over an eighteen-month period by "small, medium and large market newspapers—front pages only—and network TV morning and evening news programs, cable television news, news and talk radio, and online news." Here are some of the topics and percentages of coverage:

- Campaigns/Elections/Politics, 21.3
- U.S. Foreign Affairs, 13.6
- Foreign, 11.0
- Crime, 6.6
- Government Agencies/Legislatures, 5.3
- Economy/Economics, 5.0
- Disasters/Accidents, 4.2
- Health, 3.6
- Business, 3.1
- Lifestyle, 3.0
- Domestic Affairs, 2.3
- Media, 2.3
- Defense/Military (domestic), 2.3
- Sports, 1.7
- Environment, 1.7
- Domestic Terrorism, 1.6
- Celebrity/Entertainment, 1.5
- Science/Technology, 1.2
- Race/Gender/Gay Issues, 1.1
- Transportation, 1.0
- Education, 0.9
- Religion, 0.8
- Court/Legal System, 0.4
- Development/Sprawl, 0.1

Certainly, women care about political campaigns, foreign affairs, and crime, and the other most-covered topics. But why are those topics the most covered? Why not education, which consistently ranks high in the concerns of most Americans? Or the physical and mental health of our children? Or the protection of the planet, or a myriad of other issues, many of which are concerned with the creation of a healthier, wiser, and more just society? The leadership at the *Times* and other media outlets might say they publish what sells. But I believe it's deeper than that. I believe that "issues like education, health, gender and children" are considered "soft" issues, born of what are considered to be less consequential values.

James Carville was the word wizard who coined the now infamous phrase "It's the economy, stupid," during Bill Clinton's 1992 presidential campaign. That line is still trotted out to remind elected officials that, in the end, what motivates voters is financial security. Another way of phrasing that tidbit of electoral wisdom would be: "It's survival, stupid." People vote for what they perceive to be in the best interest of their immediate survival. Well, the good news and the bad news is that the issues dearest to many women are now the survival issues of the species. That's good news because the world over, women are rising to the occasion; it's bad news because we will need a revolution of values if we are to survive the crises humanity has brought upon itself.

I have hesitated to use the word *feminine* in this book. It's a word that some associate with frills and doilies, limited roles, and outdated values. But I like the word. I use it in the way that I learned from Marion Woodman. She spoke of the "feminine principle," which she described as the "attempt to relate. . . . Instead of breaking things off into parts, the feminine principle says, where are we alike? How can we connect? Where is the love? Can you listen to me? Can you really hear what

I am saying? Can you see me? Do you care whether you see me or not?"

It no longer matters to me how much of the feminine principle in women comes from nature or from nurture. What I care about are the values of the feminine—the value of care as opposed to domination; the value of sharing as opposed to hoarding; the value of inclusion as opposed to tribal behavior that leads to violence and destruction. What I care about is that we stop venerating the spirit of dominance and instead elevate the soul of caring. To me, that points in the direction of women. Not all women, of course, but to the values that many women cherish and to the skills that we have developed based on those values.

I like to imagine a day when what is perceived as "feminine" is as cool and glorious as what has been perceived over the ages as "masculine." When words like *care* and *share* and *love* have muscle and are no longer relegated only to nursery schools or Valentine's Day cards. When people—all people—are proud of their capacity to feel, to express, to be emotionally intelligent with their pleasure and grief, anger and peace. When masculinity is no longer synonymous with violence and misogyny. When it no longer is considered a crime against masculinity if a boy or a man is open with his emotions, if he feels fear and shows it, if he asks for help, if he is vulnerable, expressive, kind. This is the revolution of values I am talking about.

"It's the values, stupid" probably won't become the next big meme. And following my own advice, using the word *stupid* is not the most inclusive, loving choice of words. But it *is* the values. And we *are* stupid if we continue to squeeze ourselves into an existing value system, instead of working to change the values of the system. Not easy, but it's been done before. History is full of stories about the transition from one value system to another: from superstition to science, from theocracy to democracy, from tribalism to one interconnected world. Going from the values of patriarchy to the values of human-archy will require a Copernican-like revolution, but regardless of how hard it will be and how long it will take, it is indeed the values that will change the story.

In 1883, during a speech in Washington, DC, the prominent writer and orator Robert Ingersoll said something that others have attributed through the years to Abraham Lincoln, but actually Ingersoll said it *about* Lincoln. "Nothing discloses real character like the use of power," he said. "Most people can bear adversity. But if you want to know what a man really is, give him power. This is the supreme test. It is the glory of Lincoln that, having almost absolute power, he never abused it, except on the side of mercy."

I do not doubt that President Lincoln was uniquely "merciful" among powerful men, but I also am quite sure he abused power from time to time. Just as I am sure that each of us in our own spheres will do the same. What counts is the intention to do power mercifully, consciously, differently. What counts is the awareness and the willingness to self-correct. Now that women are taking on power and influence denied us for millennia—influence in the home, power in the workplace, leadership in the world—our character is being tested. How do we pass the test, if passing means both gaining power and doing power differently once we get it? How do we hold ourselves to a higher standard but also let ourselves learn, fail, make mistakes, make corrections, make things up as we go along?

The next part of this book is about the revolution of values you can make in your everyday life. It's about dignifying who you are and strengthening your character so you can write brave new endings to the old stories and help create grand new beginnings for us all.

PART III

BRAVE NEW ENDING

A TOOLBOX FOR INNER STRENGTH

When we deny our stories, they define us.
When we own our stories,
we get to write a brave new ending.

—*Brené Brown*

Writing is usually a solitary experience. But working on this book, I have not been alone. My writing room is crowded with women; I speak out loud to them as I work. I talk to women known and unknown, mythic and real, to my mother and grandmother, and to the girls and women of today. I reach way back in time and ask Eve questions: What really happened in that garden? If you had told the story, how would things be different today for women, for humankind? I tell Pandora it wasn't her fault; it was a setup; she was the fall guy. I offer Galatea a hand down from the pedestal and tell her to be the beholder of her own beauty. I speak especially to Cassandra. I promise her we will remember her story, because as Brené Brown says, "when we deny our stories, they define us. When we own our stories, we get to write a brave new ending." I promise Cassandra we will write that brave new ending. We will say what we believe because we will trust what we know. We will be heard. We will turn our instincts into norms, and our dreams into better realities for everyone.

But mostly, I talk out loud to you, reader, my cotraveler in these times. I have been thinking of you as I conjure up our sisters from the past and use their stories as evidence about why, even today, women question or stifle or belittle what we know in our bones to be true. It helps me to be in conversation with the women who have gone before us because understanding the past illuminates how we got to where we are and how we might walk a brighter path into the future. Each of our paths are different depending on our age, backgrounds, circumstances, beliefs, and roles. But all of us need inner strength as we walk. In this part of the book I share some encouragement and practices to help you strengthen your backbone and keep you connected and committed to your own true voice.

Staying connected to that voice is very different from figuring out how to make it in a world that has already defined what a strong voice sounds like, what a powerful person looks like. Elevating values that have been trivialized and sidelined in our businesses and homes takes inner fortitude, self-love, and support. I once heard Oprah Winfrey say, "Over the years, I've interviewed thousands of people, most of them women, and I would say that the root of every dysfunction I've ever encountered, every problem, has been some sense of a lacking of self-value or of self-worth." What you will find in this part of the book are some meditative and therapeutic ways of reclaiming your self-value and self-worth.

What you won't find is one of those ten-ways-to-do-something lists that make a long, hard journey seem short and easy. If this part of the book resonates with you, I encourage you to dive deeper and give what I call "innervism" time and commitment.

If you are overwhelmed by emotional reactivity or if self-doubt or depression is tamping down your life force, it's a courageous choice to find a wise therapist or coach. At different times in my life, I have worked with psychotherapists to root through the layers of my childhood and social conditioning, to discover the validity of my own voice, to make difficult changes and choices, and to take responsibility for the ways in which I blame others for things that are really my own to transform.

If your overactive, anxious mind keeps you up at night and distracts you during the day, learning how to meditate is a smart and kind thing to do for yourself and for this world that needs your calm, centered leadership. In the quiet depth of meditation, I have touched on what I consider to be the deepest truth—that in the core of every human being, regardless of gender or other identities, we are good, we are enough, and we are more alike than unalike. Every one of us belongs here; we belong to each other; we form a whole. Meditation is one of the most powerful friends you can have on the journey of coming home to yourself. It can help you identify less with your "ego" self and more with your "soul self," allowing you more readily to see the soul self of others.

If you have unresolved trauma trapped in your body—your own or the collective wounds of women through the ages—it is an act of love to engage in self-care. Physical trauma makes us ashamed, fearful, and defensive. It can make us bitter, passive aggressive, or downright mean. To reclaim your body for yourself, for your health, and for pleasurable, powerful participation in life is one of the most important things you can do to write a new ending to the story.

When I was a midwife, I got to see up close and personal, over and over, the physical strength and nobility that dwells in the core of women's bodies. Those experiences changed the way I thought about the female body. They made me want to love my body for its inherent goodness as opposed to obsessing on what was wrong with its cosmetic exterior. Instead, I wanted to learn how to nourish and strengthen my body and to help it heal. To heal from sexual wounding. To overcome body image insanity; to turn away from those ubiquitous and impossible images of female "perfection." To untangle myself from the body-shaming stories carried from generation to generation. And, quite simply, to enjoy my beautiful body at all stages of life.

Things like meditation and therapy are not quick fixes. That's why people often avoid them. Especially in our speeded-up times, self-examination can seem antiquated, time-consuming, boring. Some may judge the idea of healing as self-indulgent or as a way of putting your head in the sand. But don't be fooled. The journey may start on the inside, but it pulls you outward and onward. It clarifies your vision and emboldens your voice. It will help you do things you never thought you could.

You may even begin talking to invisible ancestors like I do. And they may talk back to you. If you quiet your mind, open your heart, and listen closely, you may hear them call your true name, as the Persian poet Rumi says here:

For years, copying other people,
I tried to know myself.
From within, I couldn't decide what to do.
Unable to see, I heard my name being called.
Then I walked outside.

It's time for women to "walk outside," and so I offer some tools I have picked up along the way on my own *walkabout*. That's what the original people of Australia called the rite of passage made by young men—an arduous walk through the wilderness signifying their transition into manhood. I believe women around the world are going through a collective rite of passage, a walkabout through the wilderness of changing times, one that each of us must make on our own, but one we are also making together, inspiring and protecting each other, and leaving bread crumbs as we go.

These are my bread crumbs.

INNERVISM

Practice until
you make it a song
that sings you.

—SUE MONK KIDD

When I speak to gatherings of women, I start by looking out into the audience and taking stock of the group. Maybe it's three hundred diverse women from around the country and world, or maybe it's a smaller and more specific group—businesswomen, social workers, cancer survivors, women veterans. I get a feel for the crowd, and often I take a risk and ask the women to do an exercise with me. I suggest they put on the floor their phones and purses, their pens and pads of paper. This can take a while. Just letting go of that stuff can feel uncomfortable when you're in a new place with people you've never met before.

After we've got that out of the way I ask them to do something that might feel even more uncomfortable—to sit up nice and tall, and close their eyes, and let go of their internal stuff. Their worry, their time-crunchy tension. Their self-doubts: *Do I belong here?* Their judgments: *Who are these people, anyway?*

I ask them to let go of all that. I ask them to put their hand on their heart and to breathe. To gently breathe in and out, and to focus their attention on that tender spot in the center of their chest. And then I lead a brief meditation that invites each person to show up fully, just as she is—to be brave and open, with kind regard for herself and for the others in the room.

This feels risky to me because not everyone is comfortable slowing down, closing her eyes, placing her hand on her heart—meditating with a bunch of strangers. Meditating at all. But it's a risk worth taking, because I believe that working from the inside out—getting comfortable in your own skin, calming your mind from its habitual anxiety, opening your heart to whatever is in there—is helpful for just about anyone, and especially for women who want to make changes in their own lives, who want to change the ending to the Cassandra story for themselves, for the world.

Innervism is what activists need, and activism is what innervists need, and so that's why I ask women at conferences to begin with me at the beginning—in their own bodies in the chair, their own beating hearts, their own breath, right now, right here. It's on the inside where we can discover ways of dealing more intelligently and creatively with the outside world. It's where we will find the courage to believe in ourselves and to stand for what we know is possible, especially when we meet resistance at work or home or in our communities. New stories and more authentic values are inside of us, in the depths of who we really are, beneath the usual brain chatter, under the conditioning or confusion or fear that holds us back.

You may question this whole idea of an inner place where a wiser, stronger, more essential version of yourself dwells. But I don't. It's one of the few things I know for sure. I know it because I have spent years dealing with my own anxious mind and my sensitive heart. I have applied all sorts of meditative and therapeutic theories and skills to help me uncover my resilient inner self—the one who is less afraid, less defensive, less judgmental; the self who wants to look honestly at my resistance to personal power as well as my own misuse of power; and the self who does not believe what we've been told across the centuries about women. About the sinfulness of our bodies, the untrustworthiness of our desires, the shallowness of our minds, and the craziness of our feelings. Coming into contact with my most genuine sense of self has helped me be a better person; a more compassionate, honest friend and colleague; a more effective leader; a more thoughtful yet fearless woman in the world.

I think of my deeper self as my home—an oasis I can return to over and over to recharge. But if you've never been there, it's difficult to find your way home, or even to imagine such a place exists. Fortunately, there are maps and tools, ancient practices and newer therapies to assist you on your journey. In my own life, I combine practices and insights from a plethora of traditions that might make purists uncomfortable. Mixing sacred language with a more secular, psychological vernacular could be considered sacrilegious, while bringing aspects of faith to bear on therapeutic practices might offend those who reject anything with spiritual overtones. Just as herbs and spices can bring out the flavor in the most traditional of recipes, adding a spiritual practice like meditation or prayer to the more clinical work of psychotherapy, or vice versa, can expand and enhance one's innervism.

I love the best of spirituality—the contemplation, the music, the ritual, the openhearted interpretation of ancient scriptures. I love how at their core, the world's religions point us in a similar direction—toward awe and gratitude for life itself, and toward a noble, peaceful, forgiving way of being human. But between us and that luminous way of being are all sorts of obstacles that we can't just walk around. Psychological tools can help us confront and dismantle what stands between us and our better angels. Therapy, trauma work, and, for some people, medication are ways of getting to the root of anxiety, self-doubt, rigidity, ego, fear, aggression, greed, or whatever defenses and wounds we have acquired from childhood onward.

Psychological work and contemplative practice are companions on the innervist's journey. Together, and over time, they can bring out the best in you so that you can offer your best to others, to your work, to the world. The point is not to go deeper and deeper inside yourself and stay there. The point, as Sue Monk Kidd says, is to "practice until you make it the song that sings you."

MEDITATION

You are the sky.
Everything else—it's just the weather.

—PEMA CHÖDRÖN

Sometimes I greet the day with good-humored grace and generosity. Next day, the mood shifts, and I'm foul-tempered. There are times when I feel inspired, as if a wildly alive weather pattern has blown into my life. Then things change again, and nothing feels exciting; I've lost my sense of purpose. And there are times when I feel peaceful, content, as clear as a cloudless day. This is the ever-shifting weather of the human mind.

"You are the sky," writes the meditation teacher Pema Chödrön. "Everything else—it's just the weather." Who is that "you" to whom she is referring when she says, "You are the sky"? Who holds every passing weather pattern but is not identified with any of them, not attached to their highs nor brought down by their depressions? Who is the self that is as vast and open and free as the sky? If you would like to explore these questions, and touch on an answer, I suggest the practice of meditation.

I remember the very first time I sat in meditation, years ago, when I was nineteen. The experience of taking my seat in a somber Zen Center that smelled of sandalwood and was as quiet as outer space seemed both strange and familiar. The instructions were simple, but the practice was harder than anything I'd ever done. At nineteen, I hadn't done that much, but I have been meditating ever since, and while meditation is still difficult, it is the practice I return to over and over to help me navigate all the weather of my life.

Imagine you are in an airplane, rising through dark clouds. There's turbulence, rain, wind. Suddenly, you reach cruising altitude. The clouds part. The sky is luminous. Did the stormy weather disappear? No. You gained altitude. Meditation is like that. It is training yourself to be the sky, to have the perspective of the sky. To know that even in the midst of the storms and the slumps in your personal life and in the world, weather passes, and you are the sky that witnesses it all. But I want to be clear. Meditation is not a ticket to a pastel landscape where wind chimes tinkle on a fragrant breeze. That is escapism. Meditation is not a form of escape or a type of anesthesia. Rather, it is about waking up and then showing up. Dr. King coined a phrase I love. He said that while we should all strive to be "relatively happy, secure, and well-adjusted people," there are some things we should never adjust to—things like bigotry, injustice, and violence. Instead he says we should practice "creative maladjustment." That is how I use the practice of meditation. Over the years, meditation has helped me become a happier, more secure, and "relatively well-adjusted" human being. It has also given me the strength to practice "creative maladjustment" in the world. To stay open to the pain of others, to connect to my fellow humans with more patience and compassion.

I still marvel that an act so small—sitting patiently with good posture and a relaxed body, observing the breath coming in and out of my body, quieting the mind, opening the heart—can have such a big effect on one's day, or on a whole life. I have studied many forms of meditation, from different traditions and parts of the world. I am deeply grateful for all of them. But many don't speak to the specific needs of women, and they lack the wisdom of the female experience, the unique power of a woman's voice. That's not surprising. Over the ages, most religious traditions have been generated and articulated by men. And like so much of what we take as gospel—from literature to medicine, from politics to religion—they are out of balance. It took me years to understand that I did not have to subscribe to everything I was reading and learning about meditation and other spiritual practices and rituals; that I could add, subtract, change things up. I developed the practice described below after years of working with women—and men—and paying attention to what helped them find that delicate balance between inner peace and outer strength.

I call the practice the "Do No Harm and Take No Shit" meditation. That phrase comes from a framed poster I found in my younger sister's belongings after she died. My sister Maggie was an artist and a nurse practitioner who cared for patients in rural Vermont. She was a gorgeous, funny, foul-mouthed person, and a tough customer, but cancer got the better of her. We became inseparable during her last couple of years—as close as two people can be, since I was not only one of her caretakers but also her bone marrow donor, which meant that by the end of her life we shared the same blood, the same DNA. Maggie taught me the slogan "Do no harm and take no shit," and I can just imagine her laughing about it with her fellow nurses. As a medical practitioner she tried to practice both doing no harm and taking no shit: doing no harm to her patients (as stated in the Hippocratic oath made by doctors and the Nightingale Pledge made by nurses) and taking no shit—none from the doctors she worked with, none from the government bureaucracy that ran her clinic, and none from her beloved patients, who often didn't comply with her treatment advice or abused the drugs she prescribed. Maggie tried to live by her motto, but she also took a lot of shit in her work, as well as at home, and she also did some harm—mostly to herself.

I write about Maggie here because I think we all can see ourselves in her strengths and her weaknesses. Her giving nature often knew no bounds. She would give and give and give, allowing resentment to grow within but lacking the skills and the backbone to speak her truth and to set reasonable boundaries. Sometimes I think if she had really known how to "do no harm *and* take no shit," she might not have gotten cancer in her fifties and died so young. At the very least, she would have known that she was as worthy of love and respect as the people she cared for. She would have trusted what she felt and said what she meant, instead of allowing her woundedness and anger to harden within her. At times, she was too giving, too kind. Then, to compensate, she became too tough to let anyone help her.

The Zen teacher Roshi Joan Halifax teaches a form of meditation that she calls Strong Back, Soft Front. I once invited her to teach meditation at a Women & Power conference. Her instructions to the women in the room included this:

> All too often our so-called strength comes from fear not love; instead of having a strong back, many of us have a defended front shielding a weak spine. In other words, we walk around brittle and defensive, trying to conceal our lack of confidence. If we strengthen our backs, metaphorically speaking, and develop a spine that's flexible but sturdy, then we can risk having a front that's soft and open, representing compassion. The place in your body where these two meet—strong back and soft front—is the brave, tender ground in which to deeply root our caring.

Or in other words, love and strength are not mutually exclusive. Doing no harm and taking no shit is not an either/or choice. It's the marriage of the two that will make a difference in your life and will change the story in the world. It may seem that in order to hold your own or to get ahead you must shut down your vulnerable heart. That you must always be as cool and aggressive as the warriors and the superheroes. But this is a sad mistake. You can expand your capacity to feel and empathize and give, even as you strengthen your muscles of discernment, self-respect, and boundary setting. That is the purpose of the following meditation practice, named in my sister's honor.

DO NO HARM AND TAKE NO SHIT

A Meditation Practice

*It takes a strong back
and a soft front
to face the world.*

—ROSHI JOAN HALIFAX

You may have seen statues of the Buddha, like the one here, where he holds his left palm open, like a cup catching rain. He holds his right hand out in front of him, as if making the stop gesture. In Sanskrit, these hand gestures are called *mudras*. In the Buddhist and yogic traditions mudras are used to evoke a specific state of mind.

The cupped palm gesture is the mudra of generosity and compassion. It symbolizes a heart that turns no one away, a cup that can hold the world. In Christian terms, it is the gesture of *agape*, the highest form of love. It is the "do no harm" gesture.

The stop gesture is the mudra of fearlessness. It is said that the historical Buddha made this gesture upon gaining enlightenment, indicating that even if we are confused, unhappy, or hurt, we can have a fearless spirit and a dignified strength. It is the "take no shit" gesture.

In Buddhist iconography, these two mudras are usually used together. This is important. It reveals an enduring truth—that any strength overdone becomes a weakness. Made together, the two mudras bring us into balance.

MEDITATION INSTRUCTIONS

Sit on a pillow on the floor, legs crossed in front of you, or sit on a chair, feet planted on the ground a foot or so apart. Don't slouch, but instead lengthen your backbone. Breathe in, exhale, and sigh. Do this a few times. Hold yourself tall, breathe in deeply, and let the breath out with an audible sigh. Close your eyes and scan your body. On each exhale, release tension wherever you may be holding it. Relax your jaw and drop your shoulders. Keep your back straight but soften your belly and open your chest. This is the posture of "strong back/soft front."

Eyes closed, maintaining your posture, begin to observe your normal pattern of breathing. As you inhale, feel your lungs expand and your belly rise. Pause, and then allow your exhalation to happen naturally, fully. Focus on your breath this way for several minutes. Inhale, pause, exhale. Observe the breath coming in and out. When thoughts or feelings arise, note them, but don't attach to them. Instead, greet them gently with "unconditional friendliness," as Pema Chödrön calls the attitude that works best with the crazy amount of thoughts that arise in meditation. No judgment or rejection, but rather friendly observation. When thoughts, or restlessness, or sleepiness run away with your attention, simply return to the practice of posture and breath: sitting tall and dignified, open and relaxed—strong back/soft front— following the breath in and out of the body. This is a basic meditation technique that you can use with or without the following instructions.

With eyes closed and strong posture, put your left hand on your chest, over your heart, and breathe slowly and gently. Soften your heart. Women have been told through the ages *not* to feel so much, to seek "closure" for our grief, to shut up and shape up. Ignore all of that as you let your heart feel whatever it feels— unmetabolized grief, free-floating gratitude, love, anger, outrage, fear, optimism, wonder. Whatever is in there, call it all good. Let what is in your heart speak to you. Let it be. Listen closely. Don't turn away. If you can be welcoming toward what is inside of you, you can extend empathy toward others.

Now, take your hand from your heart and make the cupped palm mudra with your left hand—the "do no harm" gesture. Hold your hand out in front of you, waist height, elbow bent. Keep your eyes closed, straighten your back again, relax your shoulders, soften your belly, and feel the tenderness of this gesture, the willingness to stay open, the commitment to compassion, the ability to hold the world in your palm.

Put your left hand down by your side. Straightening your back but keeping your shoulders and jaw and belly relaxed, raise your right hand to shoulder height, with the arm bent and the palm facing outward, making the stop sign, the "take no shit" mudra. Close your eyes, breathe slowly, and feel the strength and determination and dignity of this posture and hand gesture. By keeping your back strong and your hand extended, you are telling yourself that you are a noble, powerful, deserving human being. You can say no or yes. Your voice is valid; your ideas are important. Cassandra speaks, and the world listens. Feel all of this in your body through the mudra and strong backbone.

Now, hold both mudras at the same time. Together, these gestures impart the combined power of compassion with strength, of yes with no, of openness with boundaries, of humility with convictions. You are safe to be sensitive and caring because you are also sturdy and protected. And you can flex your strength because your empathy will keep you from overreaching. Sit for several minutes holding both mudras, breathing slowly, feeling the balance within.

You can do this practice every day as a reminder, as a correction, a promise, a prayer. Sometimes, if you are feeling oversensitive or depleted, you may need a hit of strength. Perhaps you are about to go into a contentious meeting, or you are having a difficult time setting limits for your child or holding your own with your partner. You can make the "take no shit" mudra (under the table at work, if need be) to remind you of your validity, your dignity, your courage. Or if you feel yourself reacting too strongly, being ego-driven, quick to judge, impatient, harsh, you can make the "do no harm" mudra. Cup your palm, feel your heart soften and open, and extend compassion to yourself and to those around you. But most of the time, we need both strength and tenderness, a strong back and a soft front.

OVERCOMING THE IMPOSTOR SYNDROME

Over the years, I've interviewed thousands of people,
most of them women, and I would say that the root
of every dysfunction I've ever encountered,
every problem, has been some sense of a lacking
of self-value or of self-worth.

—OPRAH WINFREY

A few years ago, I spoke at a weeklong women's leadership retreat convened by Sir Richard Branson—author, philanthropist, and the founder of the Virgin Group of businesses. Branson is also a daredevil who has bungee jumped off the roof of a tall building in Las Vegas, made several attempts to circumnavigate the globe in a hot-air balloon, and crossed the Atlantic Ocean in a speedboat. His Virgin Galactic's passenger spaceplane recently broke the sound barrier at high altitude. When I met him at the retreat, he had returned—just the day before—from a groundbreaking diving mission to the bottom of Belize's Great Blue Hole, the world's deepest marine cavern.

I was one of five people leading sessions during the retreat, and although I've spoken to groups for years, I still deal with what many call the impostor syndrome. Perhaps you have heard of it. Perhaps you have it, too. You probably do, since studies done all over the world reveal that a lot of men and a large percentage of women of all ages and backgrounds suffer from the impostor syndrome. Psychologists Pauline Clance and Suzanne Imes coined the term in 1978, defining it as a feeling of "phoniness in people who believe that they are not intelligent, capable, or creative," even though the people they were studying were all objectively intelligent, capable, and creative. "People who feel like impostors," wrote Clance and Imes, "live in fear of being 'found out' or exposed as frauds." Men suffer from the syndrome, too, but it is more prevalent among women, and especially among women of color. Journalist and mental health counselor Lincoln Hill points to studies that reveal "a racialized component to the impostor syndrome," noting how experiences with racial discrimination, negative stereotypes, and underrepresentation only compound the impostor syndrome.

The *New York Times* gender editor Jessica Bennett defines the impostor syndrome as "that nagging feeling that you're not good enough, that you don't belong, that you don't deserve the job, the promotion, the book deal, the seat at the table." That nagging feeling traveled with me to Sir Richard Branson's leadership retreat. The makeup of the teaching team didn't help: a business guru, a NASA astronaut, a famous actress, Branson himself, and me. On the first night of the retreat we gathered with the participants, themselves successful entrepreneurs and creative types. Richard Branson welcomed everyone and gave some opening remarks, regaling us with thrilling stories about his exploits—both high above the Earth in space, and deep within it, most recently at the bottom of the Great Blue Hole. His words were both inspiring and practical. He spoke about hard work and teamwork, also about the quality of fearlessness and adventure that leadership entails: "The brave may not live forever," he said, "but the cautious do not live at all."

Later that night, in my hotel room, just me and my impostor syndrome, I thought about the presentation I was to make the next morning. There was nothing I could say that would live up to the fearlessness and adventure of the words and deeds of Richard Branson, nor to what I imagined the business guru, astronaut, and actress would say during the next days of the retreat. "Who the hell am I?" I thought. "I have never remotely done something like dive into the deepest hole in the ocean or vault myself into outer space." The lessons and the practices I had prepared suddenly seemed pale and cautious. But it was too late to alter my plans. I had been invited to begin the retreat with a session of meditation and other ways of building up one's inner strength and sense of purpose. But what would the women think about the journey I was about to lead them on? Would they want to go into the Great Blue Hole of their deeper feelings and dreams, their wounds and fears, in order to uncover their true courage, their own voice? Would they have the patience to venture into "inner space," or would that seem boring and wimpy?

The next morning, I took my place in front of the group, which included the astronaut, the actress, the business guru, and Sir Richard Branson. Bolstered by sleep and coffee, I decided right then and there to start the day by telling my own brand of adventure story—how I had spent my life taking deep dives into the human heart, learning about what makes us tick, what holds us back, and how we might become more courageous in our authenticity, our intimacy, our communication. I spoke about women and leadership and how we are braver than we think and how it's our job now to redefine what courage and adventure and success look like. How the energy we need and the purpose we crave is inside of us, waiting to be excavated and dignified. But first, we must explore a blue hole as deep as the deepest one on Earth, and travel into inner space where we can gain new perspectives and dream new dreams.

"This takes a lot of courage," I said. "Who's game?"

They all raised their hands. We spent the day in quiet meditation and also in exercises that felt risky to many of the women in the room: sharing truths they rarely shared; turning and facing their impostor syndrome; having conversations that brought up fears, wounds, and decisions that needed to be made. I was touched by how game they all were. They were more than game. They were brave. At the end of the day I requoted Sir Richard Branson: "The brave may not live forever," I said, "but the cautious do not live at all." I thanked them for being a different kind of brave, for having the courage to be real with themselves and with each other. I told them that the work we did would help them become the kind of leaders the world needs now. And once again, I saw how showing up as my true self had helped me chip away just a little bit more at my own impostor syndrome.

There are many ways to recover from the impostor syndrome. I include some below. But the most effective way I have found is to talk honestly about my own and to listen to other women's experiences. That simple act of finding solidarity is the most powerful way I have found to free myself from my impostor syndrome.

As you work on freeing yourself from your own impostor syndrome, remember that the opposite is not arrogance and ego aggrandizement. Remember that you can work to rid yourself of the impostor syndrome, but at the same time you can also work on remaining humble, self-aware, and open to change. We don't want to throw away the very qualities that are essential for doing power differently.

Beth Monaghan, CEO of InkHouse, one of the top ranked PR agencies in the country, says, "Women are taught to doubt ourselves because we don't conform to the qualities of the incumbent leaders: white men. And this isn't specific to one generation. I hear about it from my employees . . . who are 80 percent female and mostly in their 20s and 30s, and from experienced female CEOs alike. I also have first-hand experience with the deep grooves it carved in my own psyche." Monaghan suggests that one of the best ways of overcoming impostor syndrome is to get to know, respect, and lead with your own best qualities. She said when she was starting out in business, she assumed she would have to acquire qualities of leadership. "It never occurred to me," she writes, "until much later, to look inside myself. Only then did I learn to lean on my strengths, which include some useful tools such as forgiveness and mercy, love of learning, fairness and equity, and open-mindedness."

Here are other useful tools that have helped me and may help you overcome the impostor syndrome.

Realize that you are not alone. Speak up about your own impostor syndrome and listen to the stories of others. Search online for "impostor syndrome" quotes; you will be surprised by the company you keep. For example, Maya Angelou suffered from it. She said, "I have written 11 books, but each time I think, 'Uh oh, they're going to find out now. I've run a game on everybody, and they're going to find me out.'"

Don't make assumptions about people in power. First Lady Michelle Obama admitted to a group of young women that she still suffered from the impostor syndrome. She said, "It doesn't go away—that feeling that you shouldn't take me that seriously. What do I know? I share that with you because we all have doubts in our abilities, about our power and what that power is." She shared a realization she had after meeting many of the world's most powerful people—a realization that helps her quiet the impostor voice in her head. "I have been at probably every powerful table that you can think of, I have worked at nonprofits, I have been at foundations, I have worked in corporations, served on corporate boards, I have been at G-summits, I have sat in at the U.N.: They are not that smart."

Interrupt the impostor's voice. When you hear another woman downplaying her good work, second-guessing her contribution, putting herself down, saying "impostory" things, disagree with her assessment. Hold a different mirror up to her. Help her see how hard she is being on herself, how inaccurately she judges herself. And hold that same mirror up to yourself.

Be an "I Don't Know It All." You cannot know everything. No one does. If someone claims they do, they're the impostor. Each of us adds something specific to the whole. Valerie Young, author of *The Secret Thoughts of Successful Women*, says, "Bar none, the fastest way to kick the impostor feeling is to adopt what I've dubbed the Competence Rulebook for Mere Mortals, which has as its cardinal rule, competence doesn't mean you need to know everything, to do it all yourself, or to do everything perfectly or effortlessly."

Know the facts. I copied the following from an article in the *New York Times* about women in sports, printed it out, and tacked it on my bulletin board in my writing room. Whenever I begin to doubt not only my own value but also the value of elevating women across the board in all sorts of roles and careers, I reread it.

"Adding women to leadership roles improves the overall performance of a team, across fields. According to a Harvard study, gender-balanced teams perform better than male-dominated teams. A 2019 *Harvard Business Review* study found that 'women outscored men on 17 of the 19 capabilities that differentiate excellent leaders from average or poor ones.' Another analysis of gender studies shows that when it comes to leadership skills, men excel at confidence, whereas women stand out for competence."

Know your strengths. Take the VIA Character Strengths survey online to learn more about your inherent character strengths. Validate and hone those gifts. Whenever you doubt yourself or compare yourself negatively to another, go back to the results of the survey and let them remind you of your particular strengths.

See yourself accurately . . . From Sheryl Sandberg's *Lean In*: "Multiple studies in multiple industries show that women often judge their own performance as worse than it actually is, while men judge their own performance as better than it actually is. Assessments of students in a surgery rotation found that when asked to evaluate themselves, the female students gave themselves lower scores than the male students despite faculty evaluations that showed the women outperformed the men. . . . A study of close to one thousand Harvard law students found that in almost every category of skills relevant to practicing law, women gave themselves lower scores than men. Even worse, when women evaluate themselves in front of other people, or in stereotypically male domains, their underestimations can become even more pronounced."

. . . But don't overestimate yourself. I like author Sarah Hagi's quote "Lord, grant me the confidence of a mediocre white man," but I amend it: "Grant me confidence, but make me earn it through excellence. Grant me confidence, but keep me humble, keep me kind, keep me real."

CASSANDRA SPEAKS

The biggest mistake is believing there is one right way

to listen, to talk, to have a conversation.

—DEBORAH TANNEN

Age-old, common dictum: women talk too much.

Is this true? My answer: no. Women do not talk too much. We talk a lot and at length with the people in our lives, but who decided that was "too much"? Talking is meaningful to women, it's good for us, and it has knitted society together through connection and relationship throughout history. To say that women talk too much is to belittle the purpose and the wisdom of emotionally intelligent conversation.

Deborah Tannen, the author of several books about gender and language, including her groundbreaking bestseller, *You Just Don't Understand: Women and Men in Conversation*, is a researcher and professor of linguistics at Georgetown University. She writes that "women friends, as compared to men, tend to talk more—more often, at greater length and about more personal topics. But that's private speaking—conversations that negotiate and strengthen personal relationships." She goes on to say that her research, as well as many other studies, have "also shown that men tend to talk far more than women in what might be called public speaking—formal business-focused contexts, like meetings."

In a now-classic study done at university faculty meetings, Barbara and Gene Eakins found that "the longest comment by a woman . . . was shorter than the shortest comment by a man." And it's not just in meetings where men talk more and longer than women. From bars and bleachers to media panels and the halls of government, it's men who do more of the talking. This has been going on for a long, long time—women being accused of talking too much, even as men often dominate conversations, interrupt, mansplain, and do more of the sum total of all human talking. Journalist and author Nichi Hodgson writes, "It's notable that the practice of filibustering—talking irrelevantly at length to prevent a political bill being passed—was devised by men (the orator Cato, against Julius Caesar, in the first instance)."

Then why the accusation that women talk too much? You can read through Parts I and II of this book again to answer that question: regulating who speaks where, when, and about what is an instrument of control and power. Recall this clip from Ecclesiasticus:

> A gift from the Lord is a silent wife,
> And nothing is so precious as her self-discipline.
> Charm upon charm is a wife with a sense of shame,
> And nothing is more valuable than her bound-up mouth.

Not only have women been counseled through the ages to speak less in general, but the kind of speech granted to women—what Tannen refers to as "private speaking"—has been denigrated as the unimportant banter of girls and women. Folktales and religious texts typecast women as indiscreet chatterboxes, gossipers, and tongue waggers. But what has been ranked as inferior communication is actually critical to human culture; it binds people together, teaches children, diffuses conflict, eases pain and grief, shares joy, and spreads love. The separation of "private speaking" from "public speaking" is a man-made construct. It stripped the emotional from the rational, the heart from the head. It elevated individuality over connectivity instead of honoring both.

Over the past few decades women have increased the range of where we talk and what we talk about. We have learned the language and strategies of "public speaking"—speaking up in meetings, making our points on panels, arguing in courts. But the old messages about women talking too much and too emotionally endure. They live on in tacit rules that inhibit girls and women from speaking up, and brand those who do as aggressive, conniving, and worse. The old messages steer boys and men away from "private speaking"—those conversations that, as Tannen says, "negotiate and strengthen personal relationships."

Talking in the public sphere—at school, work, the media—still feels uncomfortable to many women. Tannen writes,

> It's the verbal analogue to taking up physical space.
> When choosing a seat at a theater or on a plane, most

of us will take a seat next to a woman, if we can, because we know from experience that women are more likely to draw their legs and arms in, less likely to claim the arm rest or splay out their legs, so their elbows and knees invade a neighbor's space. For similar reasons, when they talk in a formal setting, many women try to take up less verbal space by being more succinct, speaking in a lower voice and speaking in a more tentative way. Women in my classes at Georgetown University have told me that if they talk a lot in class one week, they will intentionally keep silent the next.

What's the solution to women's reluctance to "taking up space," physically and verbally? Should women now splay our body parts on the subway, or mansplain, harass, or interrupt at meetings? Please, no. I think it's time for us to bring the best of what we do in the private sphere into the public sphere. To bring sensitivity, depth, and emotional intelligence into the work world. To demonstrate a more vulnerable and transparent communication style. To teach it, to dignify it, to normalize it. It's time for all people to learn how to speak and how to listen, how to take space and how to give space. It is time for women to speak more confidently, sincerely, and frequently in the public sphere, and for men to gain comfort and confidence in the private sphere.

Neither of these are easy tasks. For men, this involves ways of speaking that may scare or repel them: talking about their feelings, listening to the feelings of others without offering a fix, apologizing when wrong. For women, speaking honestly, clearly, and with conviction in the public sphere can feel unfamiliar and unsafe. Sometimes it is indeed unsafe to do so. If we are not perceived as agreeable, conciliatory, nice, we can lose hard-earned ground; we can lose our job; we can lose the election. That's why women often revert to covert, backhanded, passive-aggressive communication styles. But that is also not the solution to our loss of voice in the public sphere.

I learned a slogan from the social scientist Brené Brown that has helped me merge the private/public split in my own communication: "Clear is kind, unclear is unkind." Brené writes that she first heard that slogan at a twelve-step Alcoholics Anonymous meeting. It led her to conduct a seven-year study on brave communication and leadership. "Most of us avoid clarity," she writes, "because we tell ourselves we're being kind; when what we're actually doing is being unkind and unfair. Some leaders attributed this to a lack of courage, others to a lack of skills, and, shockingly, more than half talked about a cultural norm of 'nice and polite' that's leveraged as an excuse to avoid tough conversations and give honest and productive feedback."

This is especially difficult for women. But as Brené says, "Not getting clear with a colleague about your expectations because it feels too hard, yet holding them accountable or blaming them for not delivering, is unkind. Talking *about* people rather than *to* them is unkind. . . . Armoring up and protecting our egos rarely leads to productive, kind, and respectful conversations."

Imagine what it would be like to be told from a young age that it is good to be clear, direct, and vigorous when you go out into the world and express who you are and ask for what you want. Imagine being taught that it's healthy to have a strong opinion and legitimate to give voice to it, even when you are angry. Imagine if you had been told that sometimes it is good to be calm and benevolent, and sometimes it is good to be infuriated and forceful. In *Rage Becomes Her: The Power of Women's Anger*, author Soraya Chemaly writes, "Women can let their rage scorch them slowly from the inside out—or they can channel it and express it in powerful and beautiful new ways."

Anger has been brewing inside women for millennia. Of course it has. Who wouldn't be angry about being excluded, intimidated, mistrusted, belittled, accused, abused, raped, and a myriad of other means of repression? But since women have been told that anger is unbecoming, unfeminine, unacceptable, the anger went underground. Repressed anger is a dangerous thing. "You should be angry," writes Maya Angelou, "but you must not be bitter. Bitterness is like cancer. It eats upon the host."

It takes tremendous courage for a woman to find, unlock, and give clear voice to her healthy anger. It takes courage because there's a long line of scorned and punished women behind us, put there in the stories to remind us about what happens to the angry woman. In the old stories they were called hags and witches and madwomen. Different words are used today: nasty feminist, angry black woman, shrill politician.

It's a slow inner journey for most women to move from repressed bitterness into clearly articulated anger—not mean and weaponized anger, but the "powerful and beautiful" kind that Soraya Chemaly writes about. It's one of the most important inner journeys I have made. I believe that for those of us who finally live in times and places where women can risk being clear and authentically ourselves, it is both a privilege and a priority to speak our truths. Cassandra was punished for speaking clearly. Women around the world still are. Clear is difficult; clear is brave; but ultimately, clear is kind. Use this exercise to express who you are, what you know, and what you want clearly, in "new and beautiful ways."

Exercise: Cassandra Speaks

Sit quietly. Breathe in deeply. Exhale with an audible sigh. Do this several times.

Close your eyes and think about a situation in your life, in the past or currently, when you silenced your voice, or when it was silenced by others—at home, at work, in the world. Picture a specific situation when this happened. Let yourself feel the experience. Take pen and paper and answer these questions:

Why did you not speak your truth? Why did you not stand for what you knew, or wanted, or needed, or what you knew others wanted or needed? What happened because of your reluctance to speak?

Close your eyes again and think of a time when you took a risk to clearly tell your truth. Picture it. Feel it. Take pen and paper and answer these questions:

What happened when you owned your truth and spoke clearly and decisively about it? What was the price? What was the reward?

Again, close your eyes and think about what you aren't saying today—at work or home, with a friend or a family member? Should you say it now? Would it be kind to be clear, to be forthright, to be courageous? What will happen if you do? What will happen if you don't? Take pen and power and answer those questions.

TAKE THE
OTHER TO
LUNCH

To make deeper connections with each other,
we need to be willing to be disturbed.

—MEG WHEATLEY

I like to think of myself as someone who adheres to—at least some of the time—the clear-is-kind edict. I want to be a person who is brave enough to speak honestly, to stretch out of my comfort zone, to tell difficult truths, to ask difficult questions, to listen and learn. I want to do this because even though it's hard, clear communication feels like a kind offering of respect. It's a way of doing power differently. It's something worth practicing every day, over and over, in all of our relationships and connections.

I know what happens when I don't choose the clear-is-kind way. It leads to trouble. It feels like I am giving up on another person before giving them the chance to meet me on higher ground. It feels like the coward's way out. It does not feel like doing power differently. So much suffering and violence in the world could be avoided by one person taking the first step toward the other and saying, "Let's talk about this."

The renowned leadership consultant Meg Wheatley says, "To make deeper connections with each other, we need to be willing to be disturbed." But how disturbed are we willing to be? How disturbed am I willing to be? That's a question I began asking myself after I had put together several Women & Power conferences. From the very first conference, we chose to bring speakers to the stage who would disturb the waters around questions of race and privilege. I figured that if we had the audacity to claim that women might do power differently, we also had the responsibility to orchestrate brave conversations between women of color and white women. That willingness to be disturbed has led to deep and important connections across race between thousands of women, myself included. We've disturbed other waters, too—actively seeking out diversity, including speakers and participants from around the world, different traditions, religions, abilities, genders, and sexualities.

I have my mother to thank for my baked-in willingness to be disturbed around issues of difference and injustice. I learned at her knee that we live in a society conditioned to privilege only some kinds of people, and that it was my duty to try to disrupt the fallacy of that worldview. She taught me to do this around all sorts of differences, especially race, religion, and nationality. But what about when someone has a different point of view? Or votes for a different candidate? Or disagrees about a passionately held issue? This kind of difference did not get the same kind of treatment in my family. My mother may have shunned most forms of bigotry and tribalism, but she was narrow-minded and uncharitable when it came to what you stood for or how you voted.

One year, as we were wrapping up inviting speakers to a Women & Power conference—the one featuring the Nobel Peace Prize winners—I had an uncomfortable realization: I was being guided not only by mother's better instincts but also by her intolerance. Why had I never invited women speakers who held differing political beliefs or who did not share my outlook on issues I cared about? Did I not want to build bridges of connection with them? Was I not willing to be disturbed by those kinds of conversations? Wasn't that exclusion also an act of bigotry, a way of turning one group of people into the demonized "other"? How would we ever write a brave new ending to the human story if we included only some women, with certain beliefs?

Here we were, creating a conference based on the premise that women leaders were doing things differently—that they were being less divisive and more inclusive, less combative and more communicative—and yet we were leaving a big chunk of women out of the conversation. So I asked myself the question that Meg Wheatley asks her clients: Was I willing to be disturbed by a difficult conversation in order to make a deeper connection? And what conversation would disturb me (and probably others in the audience) the most? It didn't take me long to come up with an answer.

I had recently seen a documentary film about twelve women

from Boston who were heads of major pro-life and pro-choice organizations. They had started meeting secretly after an abortion clinic was bombed and several people were murdered. They knew that something was terribly wrong; neither group believed violence was the way to solve anything. They feared they were part of the problem, and they wanted to be part of a solution where well-meaning people stopped demonizing one another. They decided to meet informally—not so that anyone's mind would be changed on the subject of reproductive rights, but so that they could find a way to respect and even love each other; so that they could be part of the cessation of violence—in their own hearts, in their city, and in the world.

This was the difficult conversation I wanted to be in. I invited the women from Boston to come to the conference, sit on the stage, and model a clear-is-kind way of being together. To show us how to do what the poet Rumi advises: "Out beyond ideas of wrongdoing and rightdoing," he writes, "there is a field. I'll meet you there."

The conference began with speeches from the Nobel laureates. They told thrilling stories about their work for peace in hot spots around the world. Then the women from Boston sat on the stage and talked about how they had become friends. How, although they all were still passionately involved in their causes, over the years they had developed deep and abiding love for one another, had helped one another through personal losses, had celebrated their children's graduations and weddings. They said they had put aside their differences as an alternative to the violence that had wracked their city. They had done this through the simple act of speaking honestly, listening patiently, working through their complex and conflicted feelings, and, over time, humanizing one another.

While the Nobel Peace Prize laureates represented big, global issues, the women from Boston brought the subject home and broke it down into something less dramatic but, if you ask me, more challenging. Many women in the audience were moved by the conversation; others were not. Some could not understand how friendships between a few people could amount to real change. Others were angered by the tacit legitimacy given to a worldview that deeply offended them. I was genuinely surprised by those who rejected the premise of conversation as a way not to change minds but to link hearts.

The conversation I had witnessed onstage motivated me to work on my own propensity to otherize. I became keenly aware of my knee-jerk reaction to people with different political views or social values. I decided to do what the women from Boston did on a smaller scale. I sought out people with whom I disagreed on a variety of subjects and invited them to lunch. I began calling my experiment "Take the Other to Lunch." I started with a person at work with whom I often disagreed, and I moved up the "other" ladder slowly: a neighbor who had signs posted in his yard for candidates I would never vote for, a relative opposed to gay marriage. My final challenge was lunch with a woman running for state office on a pro-life platform. These people were my "others." I was theirs. What brought us together was a willingness to meet in the field beyond knee-jerk reactivity.

Based on these experiences, I came up with guidelines and ground rules for taking the other to lunch. If you feel so inclined, you can use the following guide to help you approach any difficult conversation—at home, or work, or in the bigger world.

Goal. To better understand someone with whom you disagree on a specific subject; to soften your stance toward a person with whom you are in conflict; or to get to know a person from a group (religion, race, sexual orientation, issue-based organization, etc.) you don't understand or have negatively stereotyped.

Invite. Anyone you find yourself judging, rejecting, and speaking against because of beliefs that differ from yours, even if you barely know the person. Sometimes it's easier to start with someone with whom you have no baggage; for example, not a family member, colleague, or next-door neighbor. You may seek out that person because of a specific issue you want to view from a different perspective, or the invitation may arise spontaneously during a conversation. For example, I decided I needed to understand the issue of abortion from the point of view of a woman whose opinion differed from mine. I wanted to know why she felt as she did—what in her life, her experience, her values informed her outlook. I got in touch with the head of a local organization. I explained who I was, how I wanted to understand the issue of abortion from her point of view, and I wondered if she was interested in hearing my views and answering some of my questions. I explained that I was not interested in changing her mind or having mine changed. I just wanted to gain respect for her as a person, and to see if she might want to do the same with me.

Do not invite. Don't choose bigots, extremists, or those espousing violence, and don't waste your time with someone who shows no interest in being even a little open-minded. If you have to drag someone into the field with you, you probably shouldn't.

How to invite. Offer an honest, transparent invitation to a person you think might be willing to engage in a nonhostile, open-minded conversation. Explain that you'd like to get to know and understand the person better. Ask if they would like to do the same with you. Tell them that this is not an opportunity to argue, dominate, or prevail. I have used lines like, "I already know what I think; I want to know what you think." Or "I want to understand the issue from all sides." Sometimes I recite the poem fragment from Rumi as an invitation: "Out beyond ideas of wrongdoing and rightdoing, there is a field. I'll meet you there."

Sometimes, if I think the person has a sense of humor, I use this line from Anne Lamott: "You can safely assume you've created God in your own image when it turns out that God hates all the same people you do."

Ground Rules. Allow your guest to choose the restaurant where you will meet. Before you begin your conversation, agree on the following, or make your own ground rules together.

- Don't make assumptions.
- Don't persuade, defend, or interrupt.
- Don't leap to conclusions; avoid unfounded theories; try not to

use blanket statements, i.e., phrases that contain the words "you people always" or "we never."

- Be curious; be conversational; be open and real.
- Listen, listen, listen.
- When a point of unyielding disagreement arises, say, "I hear you," and leave it at that.

Conversation Icebreakers. These questions can act as prompts for deeper conversations:

- What is going on in the world in general or around a specific issue that deeply concerns you?
- What are your fears and your hopes for yourself, your children, your family, your company, your country?
- Tell me something of your life experiences—your childhood, your work, your struggles, your losses, your dreams—so that I might better understand your views. Ask me some questions you have always wanted to ask someone from the "other side."
- If the lunch goes well, you can end with this: What can each of us do in our circle of friends and family to encourage this kind of outreach, listening, and mutual respect?

Measuring Your Success. What might happen at your lunch? Will the heavens open while "We Are the World" plays over the restaurant's sound system? No. Differences between people do not magically melt over lunch. Reaching across long-held beliefs is a slow and difficult process that takes time. A lunch is a first step. If there is general goodwill between you and your lunch-mate, you may want to have several lunches and continue to build respect and to humanize each other over time. Here's how to know if you are making progress:

- It becomes less important to you to change a person's opinion and more important to respect diversity of thought, philosophy, and beliefs.
- You find yourself engaging less in knee-jerk assumptions and uninformed talk that spreads divisiveness.
- Your ability to relate, compromise, and work with all sorts of people increases.
- You become more interested in walking the path of tolerance, love, and justice in your own corner of the world than in making grand judgmental statements about large swaths of people. Walking the talk becomes a purposeful and exciting way of life.

FLIP THE
SCRIPT

One person plus one typewriter

constitutes a movement.

—PAULI MURRAY

You may never have heard of Pauli Murray, but we all should know her name. She was a poet, writer, activist, labor organizer, legal theorist, Episcopal priest, and the first African American to earn a doctor of jurisprudence at Yale. She was close friends with Eleanor Roosevelt and a founder of the National Organization for Women. She was ahead of her time at all times in her life, challenging preconceived notions, articulating new rules that would go on to become the foundations of laws, organizations, and movements.

What inspires me most about Pauli Murray is her insistence that anyone can be a change agent. You don't have to join an organization, attend a rally, or proclaim your allegiance to a party or a philosophy. Murray says that one person with a typewriter (I am sure today she'd be using a computer) constitutes a movement. I say that one person with her own voice—written, spoken, cried, yelled, sung—can change the story. Every day, in big and small ways, we can do this. We can offer a kind word to a stranger or send a supportive email to a colleague. We can deliver a setting-the-record-straight rant, or an apology long in the coming or right in the moment. We can dream up and circulate new lists to augment the classics; new names to replenish the ones we overquote, overlionize, overcelebrate; new scripts to replace the ones holding us all back.

In several of the stories in Part I and Part II of this book, I write about the power of knowing those old stories and becoming aware of what we value in them and what we don't. There is also power in offering alternatives. Here are some ways of "flipping the script"—ways of using a singular voice to constitute a movement, as Pauli Murray would say.

KNOW HER NAME

In Part I, I mentioned a few women whose names I believe we should know. Their stories begin as many classic tales do—with conflict and danger—but they have brave new endings. They end not with vengeance or self-aggrandizement, but with kindness and care. Knowing their names and telling their stories inspires others to be strong and open, to do power differently, to rewrite the hero myth. Even something as seemingly small as quoting women has large ramifications. When we highlight women's intelligence and inspiration, we help end the dominance of only one kind of intelligence, one kind of inspiration, and one entitled gender.

Exercise: Know Her Name

Think of the qualities in a person that motivate you, move you, make you want to write your own brave new ending. Search for the names and stories of people who exemplify those qualities.

Create lists of people, known and unknown, historical and current, whose lives inspire you. Make sure that more than half of those people are women. Refer to those lists for validation and inspiration. Circulate the lists. Be "one person plus one typewriter" changing the way the story ends.

When you quote someone—an author, an adventurer, a leader, an inventor—see if you can find a quote from a woman. You may have to look a little harder, but it's worth it. You don't have to do this every time, but do it often enough to prove to yourself and others that throughout history, in every field, women have been doing brave work, making innovative discoveries, and having brilliant insights into human nature.

THE GREATEST BOOKS

Check out the lists in "The Greatest Books" chapter from Part I. Consider making your own lists. You can also apply this exercise to films, television shows, paintings, songs, etc. Give your lists interesting titles. I don't like using language like the Greatest Books of All Time or the Best Songs Ever Written. Greatest and best, according to whom? I prefer making lists of the books that changed my life from childhood onward, or the memoirs that helped me become more comfortable in my own skin. Come up with your own.

When making the following lists, it was fascinating to observe how I second-guessed some of my choices; how, at first, I included titles because I thought I should, because that's what a "smart person" or a "cool person" would choose. Winnowing down the lists to the books that have *truly* changed my life was an exercise in values clarification and personhood validation. Some of the books on my lists appear in traditional "greatest books" lists, but some have probably never made it to any such list. For example, I chose a book to add to my "15 Memoirs" list because it is my favorite book about the art and practice of cooking. Why wouldn't I include that instead of some of the memoirs I left off the list—books written by rock stars and mountain climbers? Yes, I loved those books, too, but for me, to cook is to live. To cook or not to cook, that is the question. Or at least, it's *my* question.

Make your lists be about the perennial questions and quests that move you. Here are mine:

20 BOOKS THAT CHANGED MY LIFE FROM CHILDHOOD ONWARD . . .

1. *Charlotte's Web* by E. B. White
2. The *Little House* Books by Laura Ingalls Wilder
3. *Little Women* by Louisa May Alcott
4. *To Kill a Mockingbird* by Harper Lee
5. *Steppenwolf* by Hermann Hesse
6. *Jane Eyre* by Charlotte Brontë

7. *Middlemarch* by George Eliot
8. *A Room of One's Own* by Virginia Woolf
9. *Anna Karenina* by Leo Tolstoy
10. *The Marriages Between Zones Three, Four and Five* by Doris Lessing
11. *Turtle Island* by Gary Snyder
12. *The Power of Myth* by Joseph Campbell with Bill Moyers
13. *The Creation of Patriarchy* by Gerda Lerner
14. *Revolution from Within: A Book of Self-Esteem* by Gloria Steinem
15. *In a Different Voice* by Carol Gilligan
16. *Beloved* by Toni Morrison
17. *The Essential Rumi* Translated by Coleman Barks
18. *Devotions* by Mary Oliver
19. *A New Earth* by Eckhart Tolle
20. *Shambhala: The Sacred Path of the Warrior* by Chögyam Trungpa

15 MEMOIRS THAT HELPED ME BECOME MORE COMFORTABLE IN MY OWN SKIN

1. *First They Killed My Father* by Loung Ung
2. *Paula* by Isabel Allende
3. *The Liars' Club* by Mary Karr
4. *I Know Why the Caged Bird Sings* by Maya Angelou
5. *The Glass Castle* by Jeannette Walls
6. *The Color of Water* by James McBride
7. *Tender at the Bone* by Ruth Reichl
8. *The Seven Storey Mountain* by Thomas Merton

9. *Night* by Elie Wiesel
10. *Man's Search for Meaning* by Viktor Frankl
11. *The Woman Warrior* by Maxine Hong Kingston
12. *Hunger* by Roxane Gay
13. *Angela's Ashes* by Frank McCourt
14. *Dust Tracks on a Road* by Zora Neale Hurston
15. *Memories, Dreams, Reflections* by Carl Jung

Here are some ways to create your own new lists:

Take an inventory. Before writing your new lists, spend time examining the books in your house, the music saved on your devices, the poetry you enjoy, the memoirs you love, the self-help titles that have gotten you through hard times, the works of nonfiction that wake and shake up your mind. Do the same with the movies and television shows you watch, the art on your walls, the videos you share. Notice the kinds of books, music, films, shows, art you do NOT read, listen to, watch, love. Observe yourself carefully as you make your inventories. Are you OK with your choices? Do you have judgments about your choices? Shame? Embarrassment? Why?

Question the status quo. Go online and check out suggested high school and college reading lists. Peruse the ubiquitous best-films-of-the-year (or best-books, music, art, etc.) lists. Ask yourself if these are the works you would include on your lists, your Academy Award winners, your Nobel prize for literature. Wonder about (or look into) the people suggesting the works, choosing the winners, making the lists.

Make your own lists. Give the lists your own titles. If you call your list "The Greatest Songs Ever Written," ask yourself what "greatest" means to you. Make your lists without any intention of sharing them. Allow the criteria for selection to be this: *because I love it.*

Strut your lists. Later, if you like, you can show your lists to librarians, bookstore owners, critics, art curators, DJs. Ask them to expand their methods for choosing what they offer; to value and validate the preferences of many different kinds of readers, viewers, listeners.

A DAY WITHOUT A WAR METAPHOR

In Part II I wrote about trying to go a whole day without using commonly used catchwords and phrases that reference war or violence. If you would like to mix things up in your language usage, I include below a list of metaphors from carpentry and building, arts and crafts, gardening, travel, cooking, or other life-enhancing, love-spreading, nurturing, or just plain old fun activities. After a while you'll notice the pervasiveness—and the irony—of the use of violent metaphors. I am especially puzzled by their prevalence in medicine. For a field devoted to healing and saving lives, it's seems counterintuitive to talk about "battle plans" and "magic bullets" and brave patients "soldiering on."

In 1971, President Nixon signed the National Cancer Act into law, declaring a war on cancer that "mobilized the country's resources to make the conquest of cancer a national crusade."

Ever since then, the language around healing has become more and more associated with war. But imagine if your doctor used metaphors other than mobilizing, conquest, and crusade. What if she used a gardening metaphor and said something like, "We're going to weed out the cancer cells, feed the healthy ones, and cultivate healing"? Or maybe one from carpentry: "We're going to lay a new foundation for health by building up your strength and immunity." Over the long run the use of different metaphors might stimulate different sorts of research into the treatment and prevention of disease, as well as change the outlook of the patients and even affect the outcomes of their healing.

And it's not just in medicine where "words become deeds." Pay attention and you will discover a cornucopia of opportunities to play with language. For example, next time you want to describe a woman whom you admire, see if you can find alternatives to the ubiquitous and often erroneous "kick ass." One of my favorite women in the world is the Catholic nun Sister Joan Chittister. Once, at the end of a phone call, she said to me, "You are leaven. Don't ever forget that!" Leaven. I had to go look it up.

LEAVEN: 1. a substance, typically yeast, that is used in dough to make it rise; 2. a pervasive influence that modifies something or transforms it for the better.

Try that word the next time you want to compliment a friend. And when you're at work and a meeting is contentious, or at home mediating a fight between siblings, or at a party where the banter veers into politics, you can pepper (cooking metaphor) the conversation with words that point toward creative, life-giving solutions, like these:

- Lay a careful foundation
- Hammer out an agreement
- Replace the weak planks
- Create a better blueprint
- Sow seeds
- Reap harvests
- Till the soil
- Unravel the stitches
- Reframe the picture
- Sketch out objectives
- Weave a new pattern
- Spice up an old recipe
- Stir the soup
- Recast an argument
- Paint over a problem
- Get everyone on board
- Find the shortest distance
- Row toward a solution
- Map out a new itinerary

Exercise: A Day with New Metaphors

Begin to pay attention to the language you hear in daily conversations, on social media, radio, TV, etc.

Don't correct anyone's use of words or phrases; just become aware of the omnipresence of metaphors from war, violence, and sports, and the dearth of metaphors from other aspects of daily life.

Begin to inject different phrases, slogans, images, and metaphors into your speech, your texts, your tweets. Have fun with your experiment.

At some point, let people know what you're up to, but don't become a word cop. There's room for all kinds of language that describe the full reality of the human experience.

THE OATH

O beautiful for spacious skies,
For amber waves of grain,
For purple mountain majesties
Above the fruited plain!

—*KATHARINE LEE BATES*
from "America the Beautiful"

Recently, I attended the naturalization ceremony for a family friend who had finally become an American citizen. My friend was born in El Salvador, left school in the second grade, and never learned to read or write in Spanish or English. She had her children in America, built a life and a business here, paid taxes, went to church, and raised her kids, one of whom served in the United States Marines.

It took her many years of study and confidence building to take the citizenship test, but when she did, she passed. Friends, family, and her church community crowded into the county court building to witness my friend's naturalization ceremony. She shared the special day with sixty people from all over the world who had chosen to become part of the great American experiment in democracy and diversity. I should have known I was going to have a complicated reaction to the event as soon as it started. First there was the Presentation of Colors—a small military parade, complete with drums and marching orders. That was followed by a choir that sang an odd song called "Pilgrims and Pioneers," which was basically about conquering the continent. If the militaristic parade and song had been complemented by other expressions of patriotism, I would have been moved—as moved as I was when each new citizen came before the county judge, one by one, to receive their certificate of citizenship. But what really set me off was when they all recited the Oath of Allegiance, standard in all naturalization ceremonies:

> "I hereby declare, on oath, that I absolutely and
> entirely renounce all allegiance and fidelity to any
> foreign prince, potentate, state, or sovereignty, of whom
> or which I have heretofore been a subject or citizen;
> that I will support and defend the Constitution and laws
> of the United States of America against all enemies,
> foreign and domestic; that I will bear true faith and
> allegiance to the same; that I will bear arms on behalf of
> the United States when required by the law; that I will
> perform noncombatant service in the Armed Forces of
> the United States when required by the law; that I will
> perform work of national importance under civilian
> direction when required by the law; and that I take
> this obligation freely, without any mental reservation
> or purpose of evasion; so help me God."

I waited for the rest of the oath. Where was the part that asked the new citizens to swear to things like voting, and advancing justice, and caring for the spacious skies, the amber waves of grain, the purple mountain majesties, the fruited plains? Where was the part that spoke of what it means to be an American, the part that described the purpose, the soul of this country?

But that part never came. The new citizens repeated the oath, and then we all went into another room and celebrated with cookies and coffee. I looked around at the crowd—new and old citizens alike—and I thought, what a wasted opportunity to bind us together in a more wholehearted vision for our nation. I understand there are times when citizens are called to protect the country against enemies. But I was surprised that the Oath of Allegiance did not also call citizens to protect the ideals put forth in the Declaration of Independence: that we are created equal; that each of us is endowed with the unalienable rights of life, liberty, and the pursuit of happiness.

Later I learned that the exact wording of the oath is established by a presidential executive order but that the Customs and Immigration Service could change the text at any time, provided that the new wording includes some of the stipulations put forth in the current oath. Now, that would be a great Flip the Script project to float by the American public, or by any nation's populace. What values and visions would you like the citizens of your country to swear to? What should we add to existing oaths? How should we tell the story of what it means to be an upstanding member of society?

Exercise: Writing a New Oath

Sit quietly for a few minutes with a strong back and a soft front.

Think about the soul of your country—what you love about it, its deepest values, its highest potential.

Write an Oath of Allegiance you believe all citizens of your country should swear to.

As you write, voices in your head might say you are being too idealistic or "soft." Stop writing. Put your hand on your heart again. Breathe. Return to what is true for you. Begin again.

LEGACY

There are all too few heroes
with a romantic heart and a fun-loving nature.

—ISABEL ALLENDE

Years ago I was asked to speak at a gathering of world religious leaders in dialogue with international scientists in Austria. This was an odd invitation for me to receive, as I am neither a religious leader nor an international scientist. The letter, on embossed stationary, regaled me with the great import of the meeting and listed the other speakers who had agreed to attend, including the Dalai Lama, the imam of a leading mosque in Egypt, the head of the Russian Orthodox Church, a noted rabbi from England, the architect Frank Gehry, a couple of Nobel Prize–winning scientists, and a bunch of other leaders, all men.

Only two women had been invited: Isabel Allende, the Chilean novelist, and me. Why the two of us, I wondered, neither of us being affiliated with a religion nor having made scientific discoveries of any kind whatsoever? This still remains a mystery, but I agreed to attend because of the unusual pairing of the Dalai Lama and Isabel Allende, and also because of the conference setting. It was to take place in a medieval monastery on the romantic-sounding Danube River.

After accepting the invitation, I received information about the conference structure and its theme. Each presenter was to give a thirty-minute talk answering the question, What Will Your Legacy Be? What prizes and honors had we received? What accomplishments were we most proud of? What legacy did we most want future generations to know us by?

My first reaction to this assignment was one of bewilderment. Legacy? I had never given a moment's thought to the concept. Perhaps I was too young to be thinking about what I wanted to leave behind. Maybe in one's seventies you begin to focus on such a question. I was too busy in the here and now to be thinking about the hereafter. But being the good girl that I was back then, I sat myself down to write a speech about the legacy I would be most proud of when I left the wilderness of being human.

Try as I might, though, I could not conjure up concern about how others would remember me, or my work, after I died. What kept coming to me were the instructions I had received in my twenties when I was a backpacker. Wilderness hikers are told to "leave no trace" when they depart from a campsite. They are told to think not of themselves but of future hikers, and even future generations who will also want to experience wild nature. *Leave no trace*—that's what I wanted to say in my thirty minutes in response to the question, What Will Your Legacy Be? It's not that I didn't care about my work and my art and my personhood while being here. I did. But after I was gone, it didn't matter to me if I was registered as a "special person" in the book of humanity.

I've spent a good deal of my life trying to loosen the grip of that clawing need to be someone special. Ego aggrandizement and self-promotion make for an exhausting way of life, one that isolates us from others and never delivers on its promise of happiness. We all suffer from it—the craving to stand out, the sinking feeling of being less than, the aggressive impulse to be better than, to be right, to be on top. That's the miserly ego at work. That's the part of me I have prayed to be released from—for my own sake and for the sake of those around me. So the last thing I wanted to focus on in a speech for a gathering of world religious leaders was how to leave behind my ego's footprint in the sands of history.

If I were to leave any trace, perhaps it would be a waft of wisdom or humor or love, like the scent of a lilac bush when a breeze kicks up, or the lingering smell of a delicious meal when you're washing the dishes after a dinner party. But that didn't seem grand enough for such a gathering, or so I thought. I couldn't just get up to the lectern and say, "Leave no trace. Thank you . . ." and then sit back down. Instead, I wrote what I thought would work for a bunch of international scientists and religious leaders and the people who had come to hear them.

On a beautiful autumn day, I found myself in the Melk Abbey, an enormous Benedictine monastery founded in 1089, set high on a rocky outcrop overlooking the winding Danube River. The gathering of scientists and religious leaders was held in the monastery's baroque meeting hall. The formal stage was set with an ornate podium and stuffed chairs for all the speakers. After some pomp and circumstance, we were seated and introduced. The first person to speak was Isabel Allende. She rose to the majesty of her four feet eleven inches and came to the massive podium. Standing on her tiptoes, she probably could only see the first few rows of the hall, where Benedictine monks sat, dressed severely in black-hooded robes. Behind them were several hundred men in dark business suits, with a few women scattered throughout the audience in pastel-colored dresses, like flower petals.

The conference moderator asked Isabel Allende the question of the day: "What will your legacy be?" And as if hearing the question for the first time, Isabel answered in her lyrical voice, "Legacy? Why would I care about legacy? I'll be dead! And anyway, legacy is a penis word." The monks in the first rows blushed; a couple of people gasped. The speakers squirmed in their seats. The Dalai Lama laughed out loud. I fell in love with Isabel Allende immediately.

Isabel went on to deliver a fiery talk about mankind's obsession with heroism and personal power, and how the focus should be on nurturing and benefiting the least privileged among us as opposed to feathering our own nests and using our power to dominate, get ahead, get more, be remembered as the greatest, the best, the richest, the smartest. She pooh-poohed the urge to be the hero. "Heroism leads to an early end," she warned, "which is why it appeals to fanatics or persons with an unhealthy fascination with death. There are all too few heroes with a romantic heart and a fun-loving nature." She spoke briefly about the new kind of hero who gives not a hoot about legacy. People who prioritize love and food and care of the children and old people—brave endeavors historically relegated to the "unimportant" spheres of women. And therefore, she said, it was time to elevate women as the people who can get us out of the crazy mess humanity has gotten itself into.

She wrapped up her speech with a warning to women not to make the same mistakes with their power that men have made. "Don't hoard power or money or fame. Give it all away. And forgive me for the penis remark," she laughed, winking at the Dalai Lama. "What I really meant to say was the other 'P' word—patriarchy. Not men, not penises, but the system of patriarchy. It's bad for everyone. It's a terrible legacy. The poorest and most backward societies are always those that put women down."

And then she sat down. There was a sigh of relief from the monks in the front row.

The Dalai Lama spoke next. His speech was even briefer than Isabel Allende's. He hoped his legacy would be kindness, he said. "There is no need for temples, no need for complicated philosophies. My brain and my heart are my temples; my philosophy is kindness. Be kind whenever possible. It is always possible."

Right then and there I decided to throw away what I had prepared and instead to speak extemporaneously, with only the wilderness credo as my guide: *Leave no trace*. I think that's what I did, but all I remember from my time at the Melk Abbey are the words of the Dalai Lama and Isabel Allende. When I returned home and told my family about the trip, my sons—teenagers at the time—thought it was hilarious that the Dalai Lama had laughed when Isabel said the "P" word. The line has become part of our family's lexicon.

After our time together on the Danube River, Isabel and I became fast friends. Now, whenever we are together, we say, "Legacy? That's a penis word!" And then we cackle like the Dalai Lama.

Exercise: Writing Your Own Obituary

Sit quietly for a few minutes, breathing in slowly, bringing your breath deep into your body, and then out slowly, imagining your breath leaving your body through the top of your head, and drifting out into space. As you sit and breathe, begin to focus more on the outbreath and the feeling of your breath leaving the body and merging with the space all around you.

Keeping your eyes closed, imagine that for whatever reason— illness, accident, old age—you died yesterday. Picture the scene.

Put your hand on your heart and do a life review. Take as long as you like with this part of the exercise. Think of yourself as a baby, a child, a young person, an adult. Shower yourself in all stages with love, forgiveness, and gratitude.

Open your eyes, take your pen and paper, and write your obituary using the prompts below. Write in the third person, as if you were describing someone you knew very well. And don't overthink it. It can be a work in progress.

Begin in the ordinary style of obituaries: name of person, age, reason for death, where she lived, occupation. After the usual statistics, use the following prompts to write about a different sort of legacy:

- Who did she love? (Write about the people, places, animals you love most.)
- What made her come alive? (Describe just one scene where you are doing what you love most to do.)
- What did she stand for? (What do you do, or would you like to do, to support, create, inspire change in the world?)
- Her greatest sorrow was . . . (What do you ache for? Write about your own mistakes and losses, as well as the heartbreaking, maddening shortcomings of humanity in general.)
- What color would she like to be remembered by?
- What song?
- What smell?
- What taste?
- Who was she, really, all along?

Revisit (and revise) your obituary from time to time. Use it to remind you of your truest nature, as opposed to what the world (and you, yourself) expects of you. Relax the unreasonable standards and the harsh judgments. Let your obituary remind you of the qualities you want to nurture and the gifts you want to give every day. Let it tell a brave new ending to your story.

DREAM

May I have the courage today
To live the life that I would love,
To postpone my dream no longer
But do at last what I came here for
And waste my heart on fear no more.

—JOHN O'DONOHUE

I quoted Toni Morrison at the start of this book: "As you enter positions of trust and power, dream a little before you think." Dreams live in the heart, not in the head. You can use your brilliant head to bring your dreams into reality, but first you have to trust your gut, to know what you know, to honor your intuition and emotional intelligence. Here are some ways to dream before you think:

Feel all your feelings. Feel anger, love, fear, grief, courage, wonder, joy. Feel it all because somewhere in that soup is your wisdom and your guidance. Letting yourself feel is different from acting on those feelings. The point is not to express every emotion—that's just the flip side of suppressing every emotion.

Emotional intelligence is learning how to decipher and channel the brilliance of your heart. We have not been adequately taught emotional intelligence. You may want to engage in lessons. The best teachers are therapists who can help you dive into the blue hole of your heart, sort through what's in there, and come back up with your dreams.

Dream with others. Learning to trust your dreams is "not a solo task," as the *New York Times* gender editor Jessica Bennett says. "We need other women by our side. So let's start by linking arms." We will have an easier time writing a brave new ending when our dreams reach critical mass (Bennett calls it reaching clitoral mass). Nurture your "womances" (if dudes can have bromances, we can have womances—a tribe of women to dream with). If you're looking for womance, join a women's group, a book club, a sports team, a knitting circle. Stand by your colleagues at work. And do everything you can to debunk the myth that women undermine each other, that our friendships are mostly bitchy, toxic, or competitive.

Dream big. If doing power differently is about inclusion as opposed to marginalization, prove it by being as inclusive as possible. Widen your dream-net. Rebecca Solnit says, "This country has room for everybody who believes that there's room for everybody." Dream dreams that have room for everybody who believes there's room for everybody. Do this with all sorts of women and men from all sorts of backgrounds. Be ready to be surprised. Reach out wisely and carefully to those who are stuck in the past and fearful of change. See if your openness can encourage them to "believe there's room for everybody." But remember: do no harm but take no shit.

Beware of schadenfreude. In German, schadenfreude means "taking joy in the failures of others." Or thinking there's a correlation between another person's fall and the potential for your rise. Or thinking you are right, only if someone else is wrong. Envy, comparison, and schadenfreude are dream squelchers and a waste of time. Spend that same energy on hatching your dreams. A good way to dampen schadenfreude is to practice gratitude. Or forgiveness. Gratitude and forgiveness are hard to pull off sometimes. You may need some help. Get it. We need your dreams.

Love. Like Maya Angelou says, "Love recognizes no barriers. It jumps hurdles, leaps fences, penetrates walls to arrive at its destination full of hope."

Waste your heart on fear no more. If I was into tattoos, I would etch over my heart these words by the Irish poet John O'Donohue:

May I have the courage today
To live the life that I would love,
To postpone my dream no longer
But do at last what I came here for
And waste my heart on fear no more.

FERNWEH

*Our role in life is to bring
the light of our own souls
to the dim places around us.*

—SISTER JOAN CHITTISTER

There's a German word I love: *fernweh* (pronounced FEIRN-veyh). It means "a sense of longing for a place you've never been." One German translator described it as "far-sickness," like homesickness, except it's for a home you have yet to visit. You may have *fernweh* for the land of your ancestors—you've never been there, but oddly, you miss it. I've asked people about their *fernweh*, and I've gotten detailed descriptions of places never seen but constantly longed for: a vine-covered, cobblestone cottage; a smoky old nightclub; an adobe kiva in the high desert; a sci-fi futuristic landscape. It's a great question to ask someone at a party: What is your *fernweh*? A lot more interesting than, what do you do? You can learn a lot about people by asking what they long for.

As a girl, I used to imagine a room with smooth, white-washed walls, in an ancient house perched on a cliff on a little

Greek island or maybe an Italian village. I don't know how I came to long for such a place—I may have seen a picture in a *National Geographic* magazine of a hill town on the Mediterranean, where the bleached houses spilled down a mountainside, all the way to the blue, blue sea. I would lie in bed and imagine myself in one of those houses, instead of my childhood home in the American suburbs. And I'd do the same later on in life, when things were tough, when I was a single mother, when I was struggling emotionally or financially, or when winter was cold and long. I'd let *fernweh* take me away to that room with an arched open window and white diaphanous curtains fluttering in the breeze. The room was cool and quiet. Outside the hot sun reflected off the blue ocean, and its heat released the smell of figs and lemon blossoms.

I thought about that room so often that I could smell it. The first time I cut into a fresh fig, I swear I saw the room in my mind's eye. Years later, I found such a room when traveling in southern Italy. It was spookily like the room of my *fernweh*.

Why am I telling you this at the close of a book about women and power, old stories and brave-new endings? Why am I talking about longing for and dreaming of a place you have never been? Marian Wright Edelman said, "You can't be what you can't see." And I say, you can't see what you don't dare to dream. I am writing about *fernweh* because we are all homesick for a place humanity has never been before. It is up to us to dream that place into being. For too long, the dreams of women have been demeaned and dismissed. Now those dreams may save us. Our dreams can be a bridge from an old world into a new one.

Remember the story of Pandora in Part I? After Pandora opened the jar and the evil spirits flew out into the world, she shut the lid just in time to keep one spirit from escaping— Elpis, the spirit of hope. Some say that hope is for foolish optimists, but I like how Gloria Steinem talks about it. She says, "Hope is a form of planning." Instead of giving in to being frightened, despairing, cynical, or nostalgic for a past that really never was, hope can be the foundation of our plans. Hope is leaven, as my friend Sister Joan Chittister says. From the bottom of the jar, Elpis calls us to rise. Yes, she says, the world is full of ugliness and terror, but hope is still here, captured just in time to help humankind dream better dreams.

I have heard Sister Joan tell this story: "A student asked an old monastic, 'Teacher, what's the difference between knowledge and enlightenment?' And the teacher replied, 'When you have knowledge, you light a torch to find the way. When you have enlightenment, you become a torch to show the way.'" Will you be a torch? Will you imagine a better world, believe in it, and light the way toward it? One light is not enough to pierce the darkness, but together we can help everyone—all people, all of life—find the way home.

ACKNOWLEDGMENTS

Grateful thanks:

To the staff and board members at Omega Institute, past and present, whom I have been privileged to work with, learn from, and grow alongside. And to the speakers, teachers, and artists whose work and presence at Omega have enriched my life immeasurably.

To Carla Goldstein and Sarah Peter, cofounders of the Omega Women's Leadership Center and my sisters from another mother. This book has both of you laced through and through.

To the women whose groundbreaking work and generous spirits have lifted me up, paved the way, and helped me find my footing: Oprah Winfrey, Marion Woodman, Pema Chödrön, Isabel Allende, Sister Joan Chittister, Iyanla Vanzant, Eve Ensler, Jennifer Buffet, Pat Mitchell, Carol Gilligan, Gloria Steinem, Sally Field, Jane Fonda, Brené Brown, Maria Shriver, Gail Straub, Loung Ung, Pumla Gobodo-Madikizela, Natalie Merchant, and Edit Schlaffer. And to the hundreds of speakers and performers who have graced the stage at the Women & Power conferences. Thank you, Tarana Burke, for the boost of confidence when I needed it most.

To Eve Fox, for gently yet firmly staying on my case to write this book; to Henry Dunow, for being the shepherd; to Karen Rinaldi, for being my friend, editor, publisher, patient supporter, and fierce protector; and to the whole team at

HarperWave, especially Rebecca Raskin, Yelena Nesbit, Penny Makras, Lydia Weaver, and Robin Bilardello, who conjured up the book's wildly alive cover.

To my early readers: Norah Lake, Kali Rosenblum, Geneen Roth, Sally Field, Lori Barra, Henry Dunow, and Sil Reynolds, for your comments, your edits, your enthusiasm. And of course, Melissa Eppard, for reading the very first drafts and for holding the details (and my hand) over the long haul. Thanks to the participants in my Indagare retreats who listened to me read some of the stories in the book and gave me the encouragement to keep writing.

To my posse of friends: family from my town, longtime Sufi beloveds, journeyers, and creative collaborators (special shout-out to David Wilcox). To the Twalkers Club: Dion Ogust and Perry Beekman (for the camaraderie and the hilarity). To my womantic tribe: Abbey Semel, Cheryl Qamar, June Jackson, Kali Rosenblum, Marian Cocose, and the long road we have traveled together, the trail of laughter and tears, truths told, and love shared.

To my sisters Katy and Jo, and the ones we miss every day: Maggie, Marcia, and Gil. So much gratitude for our whole big, amazing, famulous family.

To my inspiring, funny, and loving sons, Rahm, Daniel, and Michael, and to my daughters-in-love, Eve, Taylor, and Becky. You are all changing the way the story ends. And to the ones who delight my heart and fill me with hope: Will, James, Ruby, Zada, Gabriel.

And to Tom and our beautiful life together, soul to soul.

ABOUT THE AUTHOR

ELIZABETH LESSER is the cofounder of Omega Institute and the author of *Marrow*; *The Seeker's Guide*; and the *New York Times* bestseller *Broken Open*. She has given two popular TED talks and is one of Oprah Winfrey's Super Soul 100, a collection of one hundred leaders who are using their voices and talents to elevate humanity. She lives in New York's Hudson Valley with her family.

www.elizabethlesser.org